This Grand Spectacle
The Battle of Chattanooga

CIVIL WAR CAMPAIGNS AND COMMANDERS SERIES

Under the General Editorship of Grady McWhiney

PUBLISHED

This Grand Spectacle
The Battle of Chattanooga

Steven E. Woodworth

McWhiney Foundation Press
McMurry University
Abilene, Texas

Cataloging-in-Publication Data

Woodworth, Steven E.
    This Grand Spectacle: The Battle of Chattanooga/
        Steven E. Woodworth
    p. cm. — (Civil War campaigns and commanders series)
    Includes bibliographical references and index.
    ISBN 1-893114-04-X (pbk.)

    1. Chattanooga (Tenn.), Battle of, 1863.
    I. Title. II. Series
    E475.53.W75 1998
    973.7'359

                           98-067608
                                CIP

McMurry Station, Box 637
Abilene, TX 79697-0637

Printed in the United States of America

ISBN 1-893114-04-X
10 9 8 7 6 5 4 3 2 1

Book Designed by Rosenbohm Graphic Design

All inquiries regarding volume purchases of this book should be
addressed to McWhiney Foundation Press, McMurry Station, Box 637,
Abilene, TX 79697-0637.
Telephone inquiries may be made by calling (915) 793-4682

A NOTE ON THE SERIES

Few segments of America's past excite more interest than
Civil War battles and leaders. This ongoing series of brief,
lively, and authoritative books–*Civil War Campaigns and
Commanders*–salutes this passion with inexpensive and
accurate accounts that are readable in a sitting. Each volume,
separate and complete in itself, nevertheless conveys the
agony, glory, death, and wreckage that defined America's
greatest tragedy.

In this series, designed for Civil War enthusiasts as well as
the newly recruited, emphasis is on telling good stories.
Photographs and biographical sketches enhance the narrative
of each book, and maps depict events as they happened. Sound
history is meshed with the dramatic in a format that is just
lengthy enough to inform and yet satisfy.

Grady McWhiney
General Editor

CONTENTS

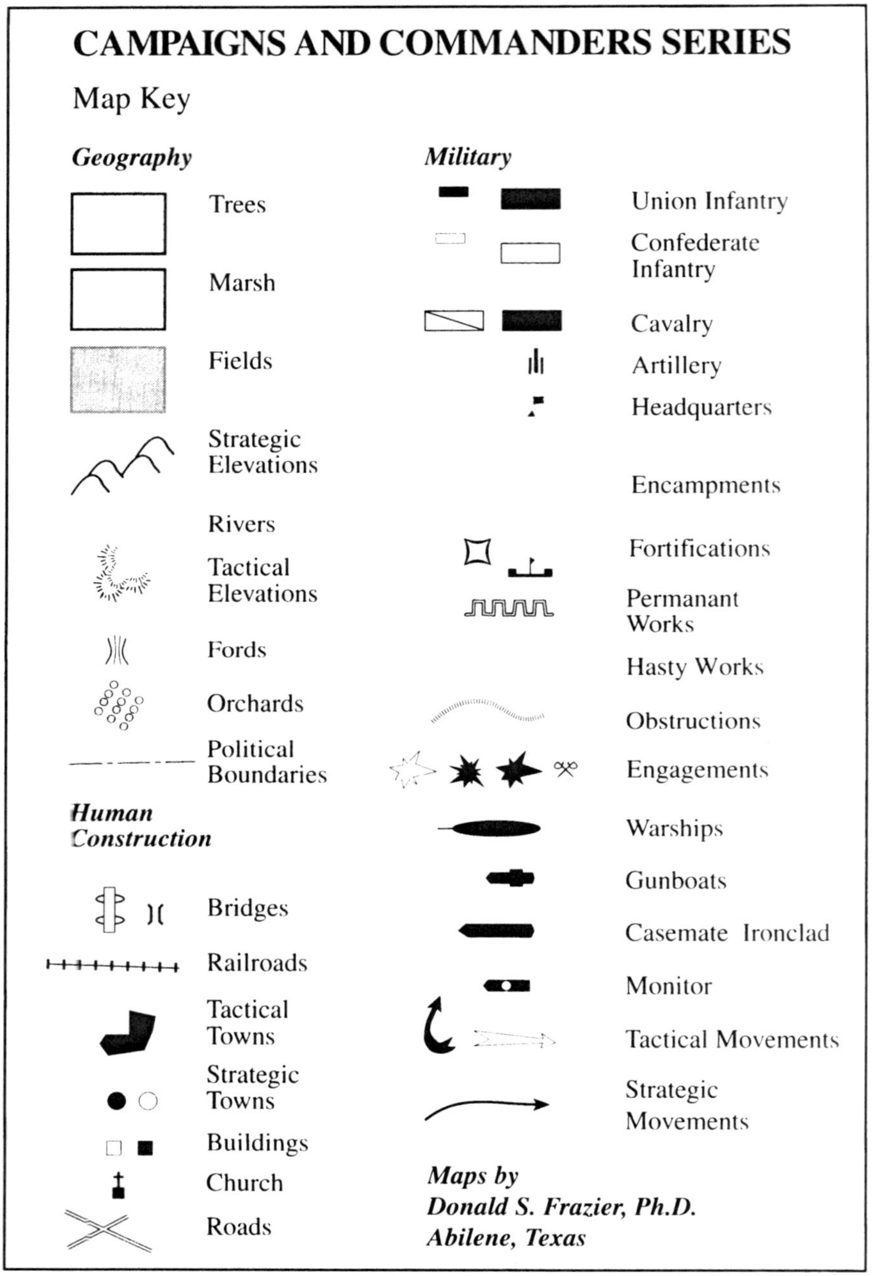

CAMPAIGNS AND COMMANDERS SERIES

Map Key

Geography

Trees

Marsh

Fields

Strategic Elevations

Rivers

Tactical Elevations

Fords

Orchards

Political Boundaries

Human Construction

Bridges

Railroads

Tactical Towns

Strategic Towns

Buildings

Church

Roads

Military

Union Infantry

Confederate Infantry

Cavalry

Artillery

Headquarters

Encampments

Fortifications

Permanant Works

Hasty Works

Obstructions

Engagements

Warships

Gunboats

Casemate Ironclad

Monitor

Tactical Movements

Strategic Movements

Maps by
Donald S. Frazier, Ph.D.
Abilene, Texas

MAPS

PHOTOGRAPHS AND ILLUSTRATIONS

This Grand Spectacle
The Battle of Chattanooga

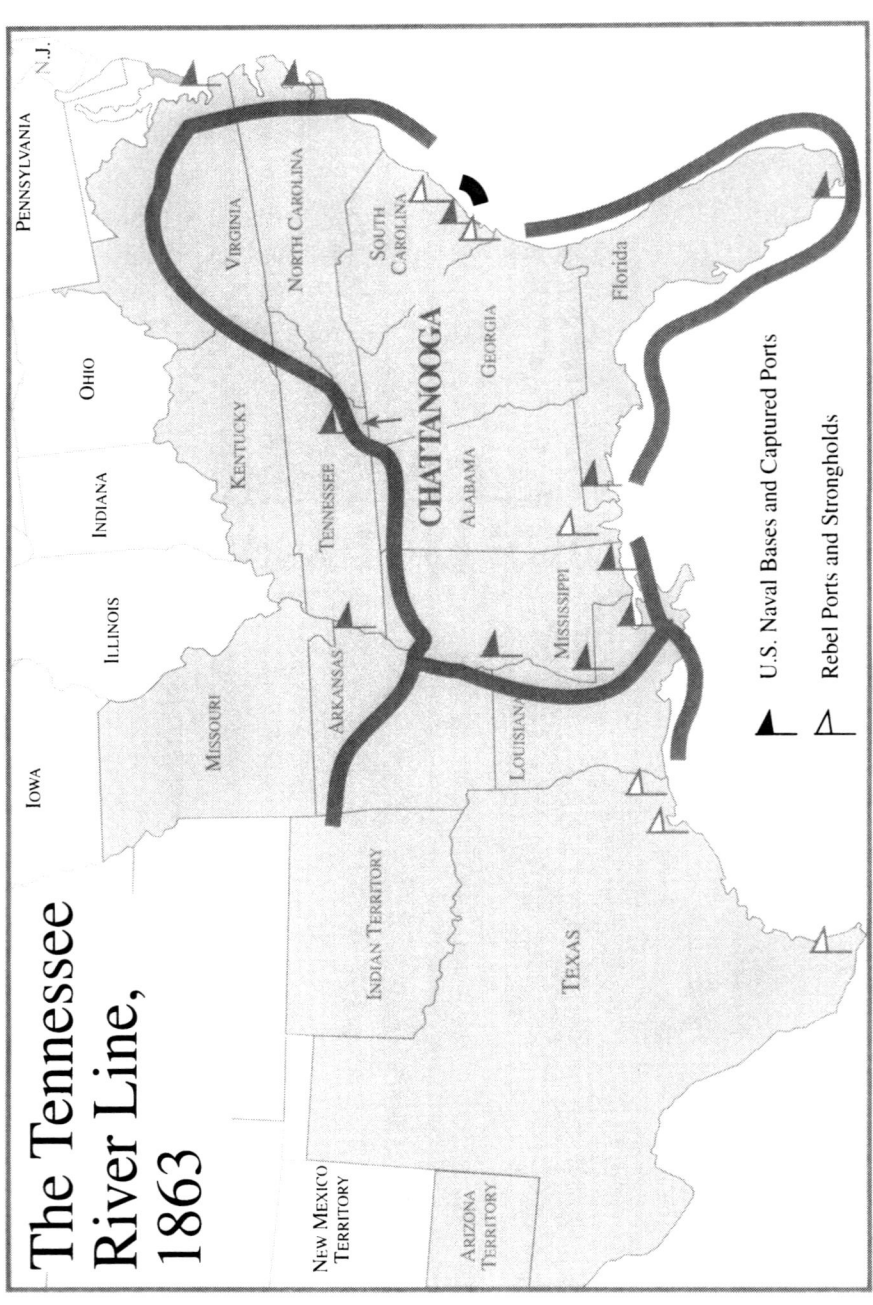

The Tennessee River Line, 1863

U.S. Naval Bases and Captured Ports

Rebel Ports and Strongholds

1

"THE SEEDS OF DISCONTENT"

This was war—war as 100,000 young soldiers had pictured it to themselves before they enlisted—war as they had not seen it in the weary years since. It was the picture-book war of neat ranks, dressed lines, and waving flags. Two years of bitter combat among hills and woods, in cedar brakes and cornfields had convinced them that scenes such as this one were not real. Broad panoramas of battle with great masses of troops marching steadily across a wide plain were the stuff of history—or romance—to these hard-bitten veterans, and combat for them had been a grinding thing of smoke, stench, noise, blood, and death in very small places. Yet now all the pomp and circumstance and distant views of marching masses were spread out before them in a picture that seemed to have come to life from the pages of Napoleonic history. For 45,000 Confederates ranged along a line that stretched around Lookout Mountain and along the base of Missionary Ridge and for 55,000 Federals arrayed against them in and around the town of Chattanooga, Tennessee, most of both armies, the sight spread out on the plain between the town and the ridge was as real as it was awe-inspiring. Twenty thousand blue-clad infantry were ranged in battle formation on the plain in ranks so perfect it looked like a review. Then, to the shouts of officers and the rattle of drums, the colors tilted forward and the massive formation strode with steady tread toward the Rebel lines in front of the ridge. There the Southern soldiers gazed admiringly at them along the barrels of their Enfield rifles, and on the ridge behind gunners clenched their lanyards while crewmen stood by with fresh cartridges. After all, this was war.

The spectacular November 23 Union assault on Orchard Knob, just outside Chattanooga, raised the curtain on one of the most dramatic battles of the Civil War. The war had taken a strange and winding course to reach the Tennessee mountain and river town midway through the third year of fighting. Between December 1860 and February 1861, seven states of the Deep South, from South Carolina to Texas, declared themselves out of the Union. When the new Confederacy fired on U.S. troops at Fort Sumter, South Carolina, four more states of the Upper South—Virginia, North Carolina, Tennessee, and Arkansas—followed the example of their Southern neighbors in secession. Virginia and Tennessee especially came as important additions to the strength of the overwhelmingly rural, relatively sparsely populated Confederacy. They brought manufacturing capacity, large populations, and crucial territory that could give the South a defensible border. Virginia brought Robert E. Lee into the Confederacy, and no Union soldier ever passed through Lee's Virginia on his way to invade any other Confederate state. Tennessee brought rugged hills and mountains and the broad, swift-flowing Tennessee River. The task of Northern troops striving to assert Federal authority in the seceding states below Tennessee, the heartland of the

Confederacy, would be vastly harder because of the need to overcome those barriers.

The Tennessee River swings in a wide loop that cuts the state from north to south once and most of a second time. The Holston, French Broad, and Little Tennessee Rivers give rise to it near Knoxville, and it flows southwest to Chattanooga and out of the state for a long curving bend across northern Alabama. Thence it flows back into Tennessee and more or less straight north to the Kentucky line before emptying into the Ohio. Bisecting the state twice, the river divides Tennessee into three almost equal sections—West, Middle, and East Tennessee. The West was a land of cotton and slaves and much enthusiasm for the Confederacy; the East was a land of mountains and poor but free farmers who were loyal to the Union; and the Middle, naturally enough, fell somewhere in between on each count.

Federal armies marched into Tennessee—or steamed up its rivers—early in 1862. West Tennessee, where broad and navigable rivers became highways for Union gunboats and supply steamers, quickly fell. East Tennessee, with its loyal population locked in by mountains on most sides and Secessionists everywhere else, remained in Confederate hands, much to the distress of Abraham Lincoln. Middle Tennessee, with its broad and agriculturally rich Nashville Basin, remained at least half under Confederate control well into 1863, while the Union forces that had overrun the western portion of the state proceeded into Mississippi and finally laid siege to Vicksburg, key to the Confederacy's last grasp on the Mississippi River. About the time Vicksburg fell and the tide of Confederate success in the East was sharply checked at Gettysburg, the Union Army of the Cumberland, under Major General William S. Rosecrans (who in turn was under a great deal of pressure from the authorities in Washington), advanced and in a brilliant nine-day campaign in mid-summer 1863 maneuvered the Confederate Army of Tennessee, under General Braxton Bragg, out of the most productive and populous remaining regions of Middle Tennessee and all the way back to the mountain ramparts that flanked the upper stretch of the Tennessee River.

That upper section of the Tennessee, from Knoxville to Chattanooga, runs down a great trough in the middle of the Appalachians. Paralleling its broad valley on the west is the rugged Cumberland Plateau. The eastern rampart of the valley

BRAXTON BRAGG

Born North Carolina 1817; graduated U.S. Military Academy fifth in the 1837 class of fifty; appointed 2d lieutenant 3rd Artillery; promoted to 1st lieutenant in 1838 and to captain in 1846; participated in the Seminole War and won three brevet promotions for gallant conduct during the Mexican War; in 1849 married Eliza Brooks Ellis, daughter of a Louisiana sugar cane planter; after routine garrison duty on the frontier, he resigned his brevet lieutenant colonelcy in 1856 to become a Louisiana sugar planter; in 1861 appointed Confederate brigadier general and assigned to Pensacola, Florida, where he changed the volunteers he found there into drilled and disciplined soldiers; promoted to major general and assigned command of the Gulf Coast from Pensacola to Mobile; in 1862 he received orders to move his troops by rail to join General A. S. Johnston's army at Corinth, Mississippi, for the Battle of Shiloh, during which Bragg served as army chief of staff and commanded a corps; after Johnston's death, upon the recommendation of his successor, General P.G.T. Beauregard, Bragg was promoted to full general; in June he in turn replaced General Beauregard when that officer took an unauthorized sick leave; deciding to invade Kentucky, Bragg moved the bulk of his army from Tupelo, Mississippi, to Chattanooga, Tennessee, by rail, and then joined General E. Kirby Smith in a is the towering wall of the Great Smoky Mountains, a part of the Blue Ridge Range. The great valley is itself creased by smaller parallel ridges running lengthwise along its floor. At Chattanooga the river turns westward to break through the Cumberland Plateau in six spectacular miles of winding gorge. The eastern mouth of that gorge is the gap between massive 1,400-foot, rock-crested Lookout Mountain on the south bank

bold invasion of Kentucky; checked at Perryville in October by General D.C. Buell, Bragg retreated to Murfreesboro, Tennessee, where he fought a bloody battle against General W.S. Rosecrans in late 1862 and early 1863; Rosecrans's Tullahoma Campaign in June 1863 compelled Bragg to abandon Tennessee, but after receiving General James Longstreet's Corps from Virginia in September as reinforcements for the Battle of Chickamauga, he drove the Federals back into Chattanooga and began a siege that lasted until General U.S. Grant arrived from Mississippi in November 1863 and drove the Confederates back into Georgia; relieved of command of the Army of Tennessee, Bragg became President Davis's military adviser in February 1864; he exercised considerable power and served the president and the Confederacy well during the eight months he held this position, but his appointment came too late in the war for him to have a determinative impact; in January 1865, while still serving as the president's military adviser, Bragg engaged in his most ineffective performance as a field commander: he failed to prevent the Federals from taking Fort Fisher, which protected Wilmington, North Carolina, the last Confederate port open to blockade runners; Bragg spent the last weeks of the war under the command of General J.E. Johnston attempting to check General W.T. Sherman's advance; Bragg and his wife were part of the Confederate flight from Richmond until their capture in Georgia; Bragg, who lived in relative poverty after the war, died in Galveston, Texas, in 1876, and is buried in Mobile. Never a great field commander, he had talents the Confederacy needed but seldom used: the army possessed no better disciplinarian or drillmaster; an able organizer and administrator, he excelled as an inspector, possessed a good eye for strategy, and proved himself a dedicated patriot.

and the only somewhat lower and less rugged heights of Walden's Ridge on the north.

There, just outside the gorge at the foot of Lookout, the Tennessee meanders across the north end of long valley that slants away to southwest. The valley's west wall is Lookout Mountain itself. Paralleling it on the east is a long, straight 600-foot-high crease of the earth named Missionary Ridge. Down its floor Chattanooga Creek runs northeastward out of Georgia toward a near head-on collision with the Tennessee River. Crowding against the riverbank above the mouth of the creek, on a lazy bend of the Tennessee between the broad curve that led it into the valley around the north end of Missionary Ridge and another that took it to the northern foot of Lookout before curling away and rushing into the gorge, was the little Tennessee mountain town of Chattanooga, pre-war population about 2,000.

Situated in one of the prettiest settings of any city on the continent, Chattanooga held a strategic importance all out of proportion to its small population and idyllic surroundings. It was the gateway of the Southeast. River, railroads, and wagon roads had all followed the gaps in the mountains, and that had led them unerringly to Chattanooga. Northeastward from the town ran the Virginia & East Tennessee Railroad, a direct link with the Confederacy's other major fighting front as well as the Union-loyal region that President Abraham Lincoln had for two years longed to liberate. To the southeast the tracks of the Western & Atlantic provided a connection with Atlanta, Savannah, and the rest of the Confederacy. Sharing a track running westward around the foot of Lookout Mountain were the Memphis & Charleston—once the most important railroad of the Confederacy—and the Nashville & Chattanooga—the avenue of Union advance. In short, Chattanooga's location made it the gateway to the upper Tennessee Valley, to the practical passes of the Cumberland Plateau, and to the broad lands of the Deep South. Once the Federals got firm control of

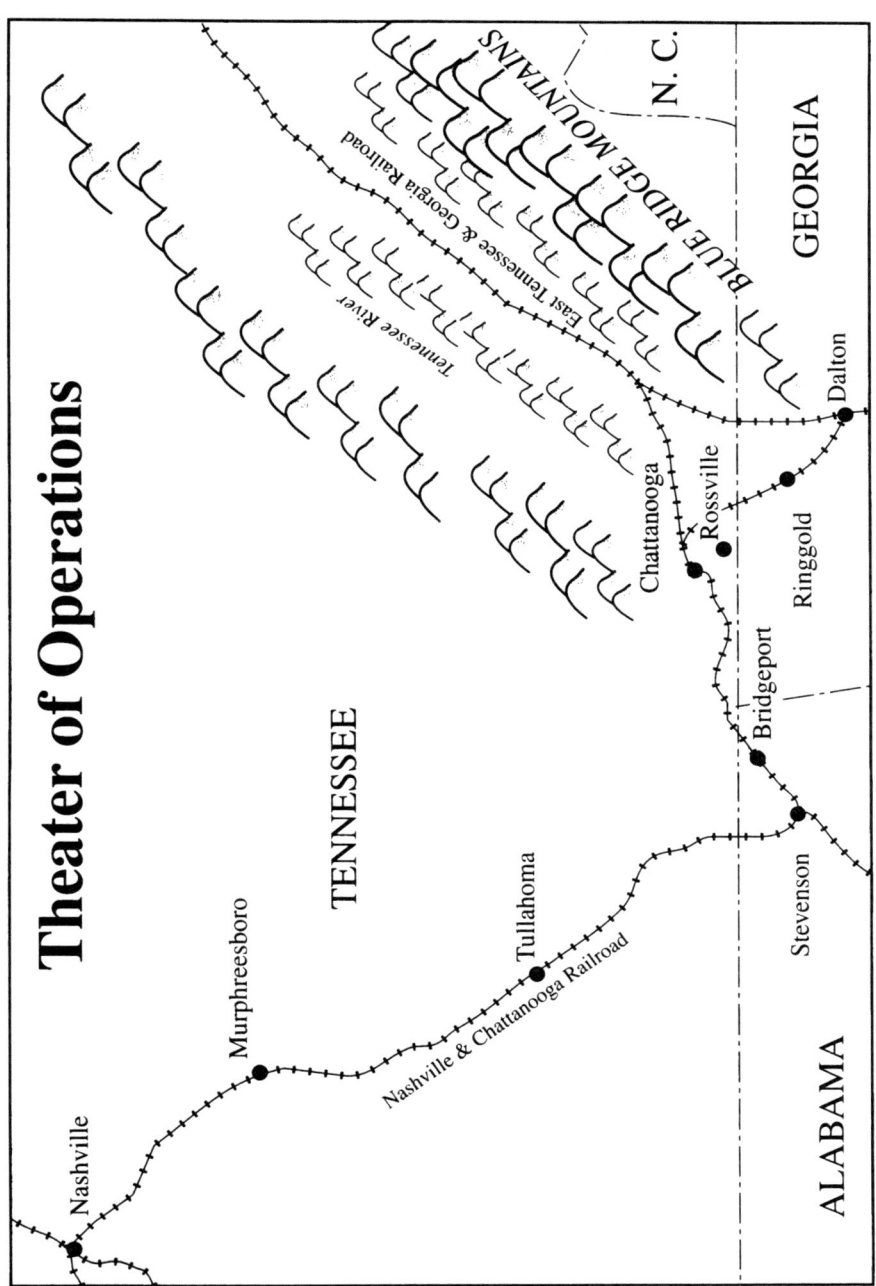

Theater of Operations

Chattanooga, they would have successfully eliminated the geographical advantages that Tennessee had brought to the Confederacy, and the Southern heartland would lie open to invasion.

A coterie of influential Confederates—generals, politicians, and the like—had for months been advocating a massive concentration of Southern forces on this front to crush Rosecrans and change the momentum of the war. The troops for such a concentration would have to come in large part from General Lee's Army of Northern Virginia, and Lee did not approve of anything that weakened his force. President Jefferson Davis, on Lee's urging, declined until Rosecrans's summer success brought Chattanooga into imminent danger. Then setting aside Lee's misgivings, the Confederate president detached two divisions, about 10,000 men, and their commander, Lieutenant General James Longstreet, from the Army of Northern Virginia and shipped them south for service with Bragg. These, plus an equal number of Confederate reinforcements coming from Mississippi, were on their way when in mid-August Rosecrans ended a six-week pause in the action to begin his advance on the gateway city.

Once again the Union commander cunningly deceived Bragg as to his true line of advance and then skillfully turned the Confederate position at Chattanooga, thrusting the component units of his Army of the Cumberland through several widely separated mountain passes where Bragg least expected him. The Confederate commander faced the choice of abandoning the key city or standing a siege that could have only one outcome. That was no choice at all, and Bragg wisely withdrew southward. He had a surprise in store for Rosecrans, however. This time it was his turn to feed the Union general false information, giving the impression that the Army of Tennessee was in headlong flight. Rosecrans obligingly took the bait, swept on past Chattanooga, and spread his already badly separated units still farther apart to facilitate catching the Confederates.

JAMES LONGSTREET

Born South Carolina 1821; graduated U.S. Military Academy fifty-fourth in his class in 1842; appointed a brevet 2d lieutenant in the 4th Infantry the same year; promoted to 2d lieutenant in the 8th Infantry in 1845, and to 1st lieutenant in 1847; won brevet promotions to captain and major for gallant conduct in the battles of Contreras, Churubusco, and Molino del Rey during the Mexican War; served as regimental adjutant from 1847 to 1849; promoted to captain in 1852 and to major (paymaster department) in 1858; appointed Confederate brigadier general, served at First Manassas, and promoted to major general in 1861; distinguished service during Peninsular Campaign, Second Manassas, Sharpsburg, and Fredericksburg in 1862; promoted to lieutenant general in 1862, "Old Pete" became General Lee's senior corps commander; on detached service south of the James River in May 1863 thus missing the action at Chancellorsville; commanded right wing of Lee's army at Gettysburg in July 1863;

took his corps by rail to Chickamauga, Georgia, in September 1863 to help defeat General William S. Rosecrans, but failed in his attempt to capture Knoxville, Tennessee; returned to Virginia in 1864 in time to participate in the Battle of the Wilderness, where he sustained a critical wound that incapacitated him until late fall; led his corps during closing months of the war in defense of Richmond; surrendered with Lee to Grant at Appomattox Court House; after the war, he settled in New Orleans, became a Republican, and as a state militia officer led black troops against Confederate veterans during Reconstruction disturbances; enjoyed political patronage from Republicans; wrote his war memoirs, *From Manassas to Appomattox*; died at Gainesville, Georgia, in 1904. Lee called Longstreet "my old War Horse." An able battlefield tactician, he was at times stubborn, quarrelsome, and overconfident in his ability as an independent commander.

Now, however, the first of those massive Confederate reinforcements began to come in, boosting the Army of Tennessee to 65,000 men against the Army of the Cumberland's 62,000. Bragg turned on his pursuer. Three times in the space of a week he came within a hair's breadth of gobbling up the scattered elements of the Army of the Cumberland and winning an annihilating victory. Each time dissent, distrust, and disobedience among Bragg's subordinates ruined his plans. Rosecrans discovered what was afoot and managed to pull his forces together and begin a desperate retreat toward Chattanooga. On September 19 and 20, 1863, Bragg lashed out savagely at

GEORGE H. THOMAS

Born Virginia 1816; graduated U.S. Military Academy 1840, twelfth in his class of forty-two; assigned to artillery, he served on the frontier and in coastal defenses; he fought in the Seminole War and earned two brevets in the Mexican War; returning to West Point, he taught artillery and cavalry tactics; rising steadily through the ranks, Thomas became, in 1855, the junior major in the newly formed 2d Cavalry Regiment, an elite unit that included such future Civil War generals as A.S. Johnston, R.E. Lee, E. Kirby Smith, J.B. Hood, W.J. Hardee, Earl Van Dorn, and George Stoneman; serving on the Indian frontier and in Texas, Thomas made lieutenant colonel in April 1861 and was colonel when the 2d was redesignated the 5th Cavalry at the outbreak of the Civil War; although a Virginian, he remained loyal to the Union and was appointed brigadier general of U.S. Volunteers in August 1861; after serving briefly in the Shenandoah Valley, Thomas transferred to the Western Theater; he fought at Mill Springs, Kentucky, Shiloh, Corinth, and Perryville; promoted to major gen-

Rosecrans in an effort to get between the Army of the Cumberland and Chattanooga, its gateway to supply and support from its forward base in Nashville. Hampered once again by the failure of many of the Army of Tennessee's generals to cooperate with their commander or each other, the attempt failed. But midway through the second day's fighting along Chickamauga Creek the Union line broke and more than half the Army of the Cumberland fled back to Chattanooga in a rout. Yet the remaining troops, under Major General George H. Thomas, stood firm, fought off Confederate attacks all afternoon and retired that evening in relatively good order.

eral of volunteers in April 1862, he commanded a division at Stone's River; in September 1863 he commanded a corps during the Battle of Chickamauga, where he gathered the remnants of General W.S. Rosecrans's shattered force and held his ground long enough to prevent the army's total destruction; for this he earned the sobriquet "The Rock of Chickamauga"; promoted to brigadier general in the regular army in October 1863, he was given command of the Department and Army of the Cumberland; during the struggle for Chattanooga his command, acting without orders, drove the Confederates from Missionary Ridge; Thomas's Army of the Cumberland comprised more than half of General W. T. Sherman's force during the move on Atlanta in 1864, fighting steadfastly throughout that campaign; detached to oppose General J.B. Hood's strike into Tennessee, Thomas routed Hood at Nashville in December 1864; promoted to major general in the regular army shortly thereafter, he also received the thanks of Congress for Nashville; after the war he remained on duty in Tennessee before assuming command of the Department of the Pacific; General Thomas died at his headquarters in San Francisco in 1870. Although his slow, methodical approach often frustrated his superiors, Thomas was among the very best general officers to surface, on either side, during the war. Both Sherman and Grant downplayed Thomas's contribution to their success. That notwithstanding, his record reveals the important role he played in the Federal victory.

Rosecrans, by then a badly whipped man, holed up with his army in Chattanooga, and Bragg, frustrated to his wits' end at the failure of several of his subordinates to carry out his orders, followed gingerly. Both armies were all but wrecked, having had from one-fifth to one-quarter of their numbers killed and wounded in what had been one of the bloodiest battles of a very bloody war.

The Confederate losses might have been entirely for naught if not for Rosecrans's thoroughly cowed state of mind. In the days following the battle he unwisely and unnecessarily vacated key positions on the high ground overlooking Chattanooga and, more important, its supply routes. Bragg occupied these positions—Missionary Ridge, Lookout Mountain, and the near slopes of Raccoon Mountain west of Lookout—and by early October was conducting a virtual siege of the Army of the Cumberland in Chattanooga. Crossroads and gateway that it was, Chattanooga had only two really practical routes to the rest of the world. One was used by the railroads to East Tennessee and to Atlanta, going around and through (by tunnel) the north end of Missionary Ridge. That route, of course, was firmly in Bragg's hands. The other—used by the railroad to Nashville and Memphis, the only decent wagon road, and, when the river was high enough, steamboats—was the Tennessee River gorge and connecting passes downstream from the town. That route could be controlled from the slopes of Lookout Mountain, from Lookout Valley just the other side of the mountain, and from Raccoon Mountain beyond. Now Bragg had those too.

Rosecrans was left with a single highly unsatisfactory method of feeding his remaining 45,000 or so bluecoats. A rough, rutted, half-washed-out dirt track led north of Chattanooga, up and over Walden's Ridge and then down into a steep-sided slash in the Cumberland Plateau called the Sequatchie Valley, whence it finally arrived at the nearest Union-held railhead at Bridgeport, Alabama, after a detour of

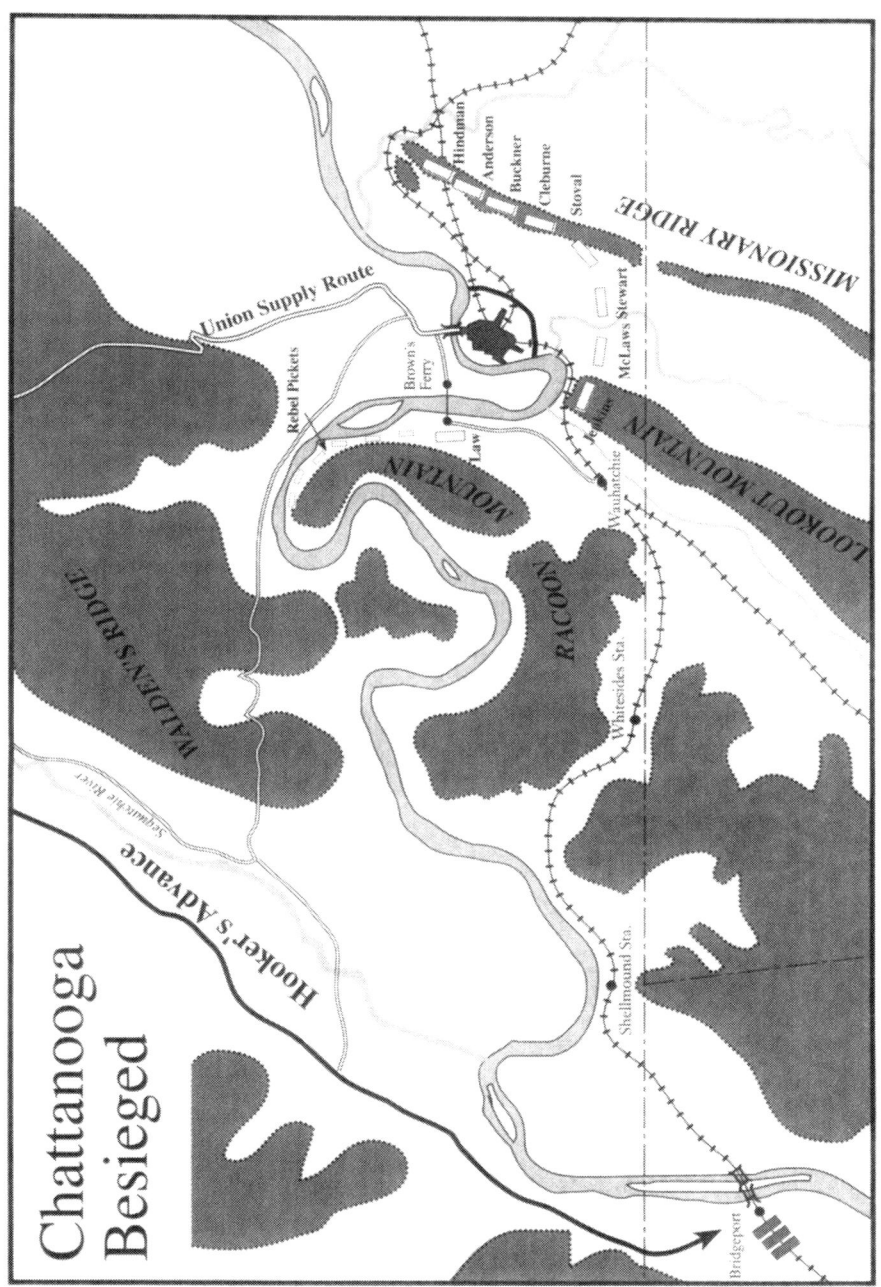

Chattanooga Besieged

some sixty miles. Trying to supply an army the size of Rosecrans's by mule wagon over a sixty-mile haul was a questionable undertaking to begin with. Doing it over the kind of primitive mountain trails on Walden's Ridge was mind-boggling. Doing it in the midst of the autumnal rains, which began in early October and kept on dripping day after day in true southern Appalachian style, was downright heartbreaking. Wagons broke down on rocky outcrops, bogged down in muddy holes, slid down slippery wet clay inclines, or just plain fell off the mountainside, sometimes with the mules still hitched. As if all that was not enough, Confederate cavalry got in among the wagon trains now and then, burning wagons and killing even more mules. The Federals in Chattanooga nearly starved. The mules did starve—or die of overwork—in appalling numbers. Witnesses spoke of seeing the road over Walden's Ridge and through Sequatchie Valley lined with their rotting carcasses.

Like the dead mules, neither of the two army commanders, Bragg and Rosecrans, was in particularly good odor with large numbers of his compatriots. Despite a victory of sorts at Chickamauga and his current stranglehold on the Army of the Cumberland, Braxton Bragg was despised by many within his army. Malcontent and incompetent generals whom Davis had forced him to keep in the army more than a year earlier had poisoned the attitude of many of their fellow officers against Bragg, convincing them to disobey his orders on the grounds that they would always lead to disaster. As often as not these generals did disobey, and the result, of course, was disaster— which made them all the more certain that Bragg was a fool, or a knave, or both. The officer corps seethed with unrest, and while Bragg tried to besiege Rosecrans, he himself was all but besieged by his own officers, who even got up a petition to Richmond, demanding that he be sacked. With limited support from Jefferson Davis, Bragg did his best to court-martial, transfer, demote, or otherwise somehow get rid of the worst of the troublemakers, and reorganized his army to break up cliques of officers with attitude problems. Davis even visited the army in person and in a speech remarked pointedly, "He who sows the seeds of discontent and distrust prepares for the harvest of slaughter and defeat." Yet in the end his efforts and Bragg's proved unsuccessful. The poison of bitterness and distrust had spread throughout the army and seeped down to the common soldiers. Not all the officers and soldiers hated and distrusted Bragg, but enough of them did to assure that the Army of Tennessee would go into its next battle with rock-bottom morale.

While Bragg enjoyed at least partial support from his superiors in Richmond, Rosecrans's biggest problem was with those to whom he answered in Washington. Lincoln, Secretary of War Edwin M. Stanton, and Major General Henry W. Halleck had for some time been frustrated with Rosecrans. His brilliant campaigns and rapid advances of the previous summer were all very well, but the men in Washington felt emphatically that he dallied too long before launching them, stopped too soon in the midst of them, and lacked a keen drive for his enemy's jugular. Then of course there had been Chickamauga. Since that debacle, they had also come to suspect—with good reason—that he was pretty badly demoralized. As Lincoln put it, Rosecrans had been acting "confused and stunned like a duck hit on the head." Within a month of the Battle of Chickamauga, the Washington authorities had moved decisively to remedy the two most serious problems of the Federal forces in Chattanooga. To boost their inferior numbers, reinforcements were started toward them from both Mississippi and Virginia. To give them a resolute commander, Halleck sent a telegram to Major General Ulysses S. Grant to report at once to Louisville, Kentucky, meet a War Department representative there, and be briefed on an important new assignment.

GENERAL ULYSSES S. GRANT

Born Ohio 1822; graduated U.S. Military Academy 1843, twenty-first in his class; brevetted 2d lieutenant in 4th Infantry 1843; 2d lieutenant 1845; 1st lieutenant 1847; regimental quartermaster 1847 to 1853; brevetted captain 1847 for gallant conduct in Mexican War; assigned in 1852 to duty in California, where he missed his wife and drank heavily. Resigned from army in 1854 to avoid court martial; failed at a number of undertakings; appointed colonel 21st Illinois Infantry and then brigadier general volunteers in 1861; major general volunteers 1862; gained national attention following victories at Fort Donelson, Shiloh, and Vicksburg; received thanks of Congress and promotion to major general U.S. Army in 1863; after victories around Chattanooga, appointed lieutenant general and commander of all U.S. forces in 1864. Accompanied Meade's Army of the Potomac on a bloody campaign of attrition through the Wilderness, Spotsylvania, Cold Harbor, siege of Petersburg, and the pursuit to Appomattox; commander of the U.S. Army 1864 to 1869; U.S. president 1869 to 1877. Visited Europe, suffered bankruptcy, and wrote his memoirs while dying of cancer; died in 1885 in New York City, where he is buried. "The art of war is simple enough," Grant once explained. "Find out where your enemy is. Get at him as soon as you can. Strike at him as hard as you can, and keep moving on." A staff officer said of Grant: "His face has three expressions: deep thought, extreme determination, and great simplicity and calmness."

2
"So Grand a Military Display"

When Grant arrived in Louisville, the War Department representative turned out to be none other than Stanton himself. The new assignment, of course, was overall command of Union forces west of the Appalachians with special concern for the situation at Chattanooga, where he was expected to go in person, take command, and set things to rights. Stanton gave Grant the option of keeping Rosecrans as a subordinate or sacking him and giving command of the Army of the Cumberland to George Thomas instead. Grant had worked with Rosecrans before and did not particularly care for him, so the choice was clear. Despite this move in his favor, Thomas was no friend of Grant's. A Rosecrans supporter, Thomas also seemed to resent and perhaps envy Grant's position. When Grant arrived in Chattanooga near the end of October, cold, wet, and tired after a harrowing ride over Walden's Ridge and through a driving storm, Thomas was not especially hospitable.

Grant was not about to let strained relations stop him from getting the job done in Chattanooga. The first task, obviously, was to find a better way of getting food into the city. Rosecrans and his chief engineer, Brigadier General William F. "Baldy" Smith, had worked out a plan for accomplishing that, but somehow the time had never seemed right for implementing it. Grant got to town, studied the situation, studied the plan, and told Smith to get on with it. In the predawn hours of October 27, Union troops boarded pontoon boats at Chattanooga and shoved out into the Tennessee. They drifted along a deep bend of the river, Moccasin Bend, that brought them to the very foot of Confederate-held Lookout Mountain. Despite the full moon, the Rebel pickets did not notice them, and they drifted on past the mountain to land as planned at a place called Brown's Ferry in Lookout Valley. The Confederates had only a couple of regiments spread between the valley and Raccoon Mountain, and these were quickly driven off by the Union landing party and additional troops who had marched the shortcut across the base of Moccasin Bend and then been ferried across in the same boats. Soon a pontoon bridge was in place and Grant's new "Cracker Line"—so called for the hardtack "cracker" that was the staple of Civil War soldiers' diet—was open for business. The Confederates on Raccoon Mountain and in Lookout Valley were driven off, and those on Lookout Mountain rendered helpless to prevent the flow of supplies by the shockingly simple expedient of running the goods over a short wagon road that spanned the base of Moccasin Bend, sheltered by intervening hills from the fire of Confederates on the mountain.

Bragg at once recognized this as the ruination of his strategy and tried to do something about it. In that effort he was hindered by one Union general and one Confederate. The Union general was Major General Joseph Hooker, commanding the Eleventh and Twelfth Corps of the Army of the Potomac, now detached to the Army of the Cumberland. Following Grant's instructions, Hooker brought his approximately 10,000 men

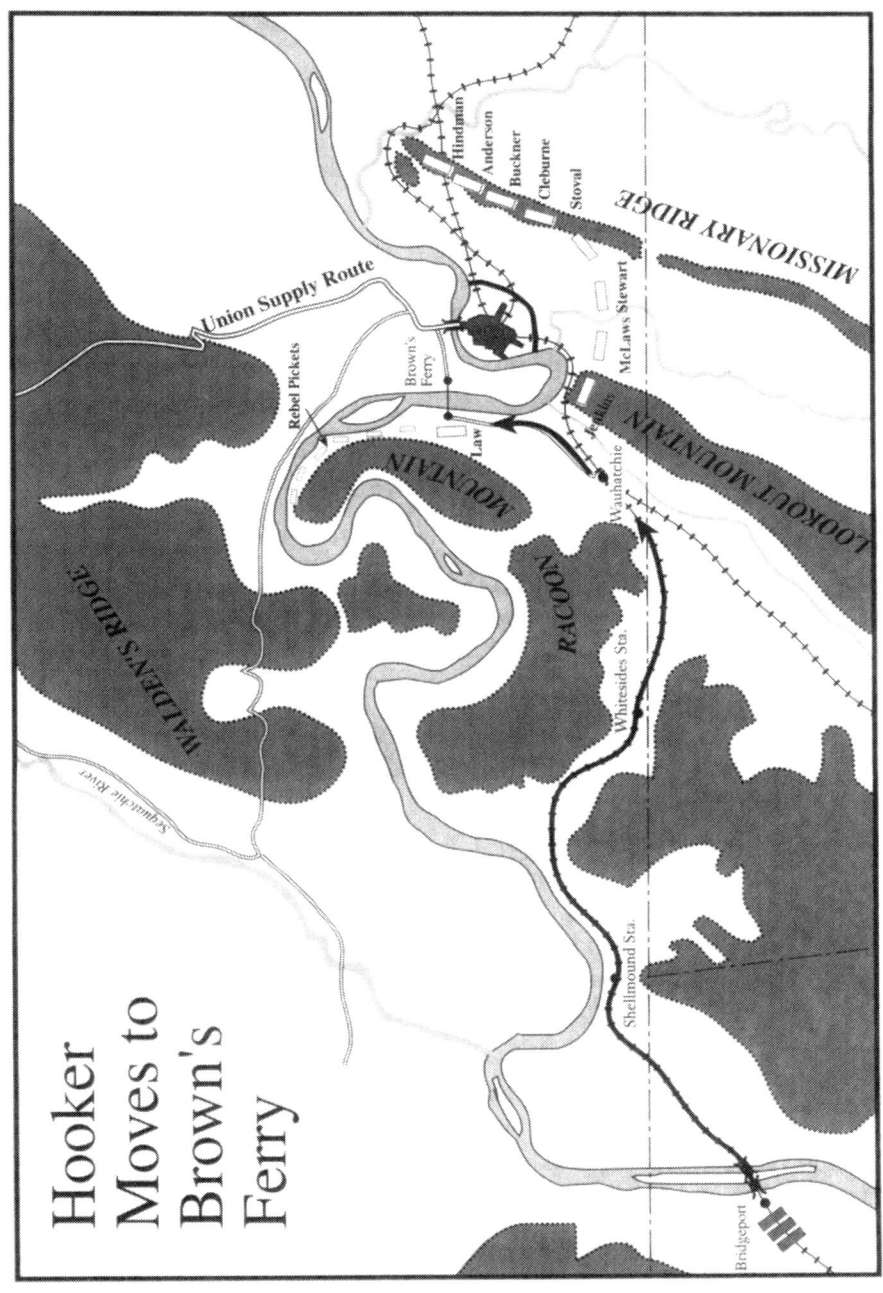

Hooker
Moves to
Brown's
Ferry

(the rest had been detailed to guard the railroads back toward Nashville) up from the railhead at Bridgeport on November 28 to encamp in Lookout Valley, further securing the new Cracker Line. The Confederate general was James Longstreet. Talented within certain limits, Longstreet could be an incredible bungler if allowed to attempt something outside those limits. He also considered himself the premier general of the war, and resented having to take orders from anyone, especially Bragg, whose job he long had coveted. His sector at Chattanooga included Lookout Mountain, Lookout Valley, and Raccoon Mountain, and the recent opening of the Cracker Line had come on his watch, so to speak. Bragg ordered him to slam the door shut again on the Union hardtack express, using whatever force was necessary to do so. Instead Longstreet utilized only a single division in a fabulously botched night attack that accomplished nothing beyond getting a number of people shot.

That was that. The Cracker Line would stay open, and Bragg's whole strategy of starving the Federals out of Chattanooga—or better yet forcing their surrender—was gone. The Confederate commander now had to think of another alternative, and there were no really good ones. A head-on attack against the Union entrenchments at Chattanooga was out of the question. A retreat would be disastrous for Confederate morale, to say nothing of Bragg's own rather shaky tenure as army commander. Sitting still and waiting to see what Grant would come up with looked like a pretty effective method of landing in a Yankee prisoner-of-war camp. That left a move by one flank or the other. A move to his left (westward) would take Bragg away from his own supply lines while the Federals could drop back comfortably on theirs. It would also be walking right into the path of 20,000 hard-bitten Union veterans of Vicksburg, moving rapidly toward Chattanooga under their commander Major General William Tecumseh Sherman in response to orders from Grant. On the other hand, a move to the right (northeastward) would be easier to do

without losing rail connections with Atlanta and would also
open up the possibility of a railroad supply line through East
Tennessee from Virginia. Such a supply source could allow him

WILLIAM T. SHERMAN

Born Ohio 1820; graduated from U.S. Military Academy 1840, sixth in his
class; 2d lieutenant 3rd Artillery 1840; 1st lieutenant 1841; stationed in
California during Mexican War; captain 1850. Resigned from army 1853 to
become banker; after business failed, Sherman voluntarily assumed personal financial responsibility for money lost by his
friends; practiced law for a short time in Kansas,
losing only case he tried; from 1859 to 1861
superintendent of military college that later
became Louisiana State University. Colonel 13th
Infantry and then brigadier general volunteers
1861; commanded brigade at First Bull Run;
commanded division at Shiloh; major general
volunteers 1862 to 1864, serving under Grant in
the Vicksburg and Chattanooga campaigns;
brigadier general U.S. Army 1863; major general
1864; assumed direction of principal military
operations in the West. Directed Meridian and
Atlanta campaigns, March to the Sea, and
Carolina campaign that ended in surrender of
Joseph E. Johnston's army in 1865; received
thanks of Congress "for gallant and arduous services" during the Civil War; lieutenant general
1866; general 1869; commander of the army
1869 to 1883; retired 1883; published memoirs 1875; died 1891. Made his
famous statement, "war is all hell," in a speech at Columbus, Ohio, in 1880.
An officer noted that Sherman's "features express determination, particularly
the mouth. He is a very homely man, with a regular nest of wrinkles in his
face, which play and twist as he eagerly talks on each subject; but his
expression is pleasant and kindly." Some authorities rate him an even better
general than Grant.

to carry out a general's dream of operating against his opponent's supply line while his own remained secure. He could then turn Grant right out of Chattanooga.

Of course there were drawbacks to the scheme. For one thing, the railroad to Virginia probably could not provide even the inadequate amount of supplies he was getting over the line from Atlanta. The main problem, though, was presented by the 20,000 or so Yankees of the Army of the Ohio, Major General Ambrose Burnside commanding, who had ensconced themselves in the vicinity of Knoxville, right on the East Tennessee railroad. Richmond had already been after Bragg to do something about Burnside, and in response he had detached a single division under Major General Carter Stevenson to threaten

AMBROSE EVERETT BURNSIDE

Born Indiana 1824; apprenticed to a tailor and worked in a shop until friends of his father, an Indiana legislator, secured him an appointment to the U.S. Military Academy, where he graduated eighteenth in the class of 1847; appointed 2d lieutenant in 3rd Artillery in 1847, but saw little service in Mexico; promoted to 1st lieutenant in 1851; married Mary Richmond Bishop of Rhode Island in 1852 and resigned from army a year later to manufacture a breech-loading rifle he invented; company went bankrupt in 1857; major general in the Rhode Island militia and treasurer of the Illinois Central Railroad before the Civil War; in 1861 organized and became colonel of 1st Rhode Island Infantry, which was among the earliest regiments to reach Washington; became friend of President Lincoln and received promotion to brigadier general of volunteers in August 1861 after commanding a brigade at the Battle of Bull Run; in 1862 commanded a successful operation the Federals. The first prerequisite to any sort of a right-flank strategy now, however, would be not just threatening Burnside but getting rid of him.

That too dovetailed nicely with what Richmond was demanding at the moment. Lee had never been in favor of giving up Longstreet and his men, and Davis never could brave the august general's disapproval for long. By the end of October he was mirroring Lee's attitude by suggesting that Bragg might want to send Longstreet into East Tennessee to deal with Burnside, since that would also put the Army of Northern Virginia contingent on its way back to Lee. Bragg was only too happy to be rid of Longstreet, and so the arrangements were made. Stevenson's Division would be pulled back

along the North Carolina Coast; commissioned a major general of volunteers and received awards and thanks from various states; at Sharpsburg he wasted too much time crossing Antietam Creek and attacking the Confederate right; after twice declining command of the Army of the Potomac, he finally accepted, although he considered himself incompetent and proved himself correct by crossing the Rappahannock River in December 1862 and making a disastrous attack on the awaiting Confederate army at Fredericksburg; "I ought to retire to private life," Burnside informed President Lincoln, who after relieving him of command in the East assigned him to command the Department of the Ohio; at Lincoln's urging, he advanced into East Tennessee and in November 1863 repulsed an assault on Knoxville by Confederates under James Longstreet; Burnside and his Ninth Corps returned to the East in 1864 to serve under Grant from the Wilderness to Petersburg; blamed by General George Meade for the Union failure at the Crater, Burnside shortly thereafter went on leave and never returned to duty; in 1865 he resigned his commission; after the war he became president of various railroad and other companies; elected governor of Rhode Island in 1866 and reelected in 1867 and 1868; elected to U.S. Senate from Rhode Island in 1874, where he served until his death at Bristol, Rhode Island, in 1881.

PATRICK CLEBURNE

Born Ireland 1828; served for three years in the British Army before purchasing his discharge and migrating to the United States in 1849; settling in Helena, Arkansas, he became a naturalized citizen; worked as a druggist and studied law, gaining admittance to the bar in 1856; in 1860 he helped organize a local militia company, the Yell Rifles, and became its captain;

with the secession of Arkansas, Cleburne was elected colonel of a regiment that eventually became the 15th Arkansas; joined General William J. Hardee's command in the advance on Bowling Green, Kentucky, beginning a long association and friendship with that officer; promoted to brigadier general in March 1862, Cleburne led a brigade with conspicuous skill at Shiloh; commanding a provisional division, he was instrumental in the Confederate victory at Richmond, Kentucky, where he was shot through the face; back with his brigade, he was again wounded at Perryville in October 1862; promoted to major general in December 1862, he led a division at Murfreesboro and Chickamauga; his command held its position on Missionary Ridge during the rout of General Braxton Bragg's Army of Tennessee and then covered Bragg's retreat; his stand at Ringgold Gap may have saved the army from destruction; his off-the-battlefield actions, however, cost him further promotion; he was an ardent member of the anti-Bragg faction calling for that general's removal and his proposal to arm slaves for service in the Confederate Army angered many, including President Jefferson Davis; Cleburne fought throughout the Atlanta Campaign, but was continually passed over for promotion; he was killed during the savage fighting at Franklin, Tennessee, in November 1864. General Cleburne was arguably the finest general officer in the Army of Tennessee and among the best to emerge during the war. He was one of only two foreign-born officers to become a major general in the Confederate Army.

to Chattanooga while Longstreet's two divisions along with some extra cavalry would head for Knoxville to take care of Burnside and open the way for a major right-flank movement by the Army of Tennessee.

Longstreet started on November 4, but moved slowly and complained constantly. He bungled a prime chance to bag Burnside's main field force and then settled down to besiege that general and about 12,000 of his men in Knoxville. What Bragg needed was quick work, but despite a significant numerical superiority Longstreet continued to grouse that he did not have enough troops. By November 23, Bragg in desperation was ready to comply. He gave orders for Brigadier General Bushrod R. Johnson's and Major General Patrick R. Cleburne's Divisions to pull out of line, march to the railroad depot at Chickamauga Station, and ride the rails to Knoxville. It would be taking an enormous risk, but Bragg simply could not afford to sit idly in front of Chattanooga until Grant's offensive plans were ready for implementation.

In fact it was a good deal later than Bragg thought. Grant had begun contemplating offensive action soon after opening the Cracker Line, partially because of his basic approach to war, and partially because of the pressure he was getting from Lincoln, Stanton, and Halleck. Although Longstreet's siege of Knoxville was porous enough to let in a good deal more food than had reached Chattanooga before the opening of the Cracker Line, Burnside was nevertheless plying Washington with pitiful appeals for help. Their effect in the capital was amplified by the president's great solicitude for the suffering Unionists of East Tennessee. As a result, Grant got a good bit of nagging—Halleck was especially good at that sort of thing—about doing something to help poor Burnside.

Thus with more than the usual incentive to get right down to business, Grant laid his plans. His program for the coming battle envisioned making maximum use of subordinates he could trust. If relations between Grant and Thomas were, at best, businesslike, those between Grant and his other top subordinate at Chattanooga, William Tecumseh Sherman, were all that could be wished for. Grant and Sherman had become close friends early in the war, and their relationship had been cemented by shared participation in difficult undertakings and spectacular successes. Sherman was actually not yet in Chattanooga when Grant arrived but was working his way across northern Alabama with four divisions, about 20,000 men, of his Army of the Tennessee, repairing the Memphis & Charleston Railroad as he went, as per his instructions from the War Department. Grant immediately sent him orders to forget the Memphis & Charleston and get to Chattanooga with his tough, veteran troops as soon as possible. Sherman was glad to comply, and despite muddy roads and destroyed bridges was nearing the city by mid-November.

Hurrying ahead of his troops, Sherman arrived at Grant's headquarters on November 14 to discuss plans. Delighted to see him, Grant jumped up to offer him his own seat, exclaiming, "Take the chair of honor, Sherman."

"The chair of honor? Oh, no! That belongs to you, general," replied Sherman.

"I don't forget, Sherman," Grant returned slyly, "to give proper respect to age."

"Well, then," said Sherman, who was two years older, "if you put it on that ground, I accept."

Their rapport was excellent and they fell at once to planning unpleasant things for Mr. Bragg across the way. Essentially, the program upon which they agreed called for Thomas and Hooker to threaten Bragg's left, on Lookout Mountain, and his center, on Missionary Ridge, while Sherman made the key attack. He would cross his army to the north bank of the river on the pontoon bridge at Brown's Ferry, then march it upstream past the city, cross the river in another one of those daring pontoon boat assaults, and move down on Bragg's right flank, at the north end of Missionary Ridge. Once he got up there, he could move right along the ridge, rolling up Bragg's line, while Thomas and Hooker piled in too.

Eager to implement the plan, Sherman hurried to rejoin his troops. Too late to catch the steamboat that had brought him up the river, he borrowed a rowboat and four soldiers and pushed on through the night, taking turns at the oars himself. Back at his camps, however, he found that no amount of personal drive could move his column forward as fast as called for by the plan he and Grant had worked out. Mud, the perpetual bane of every Civil War army that attempted to move during wet weather over the South's mostly dirt roads, impeded progress despite all that he and his men could do. Grant had planned to start his grand offensive on November 21, but that day came and went with the Army of the Tennessee still toiling along the soggy roads. The twenty-second passed, the rainy weather continued, and still Sherman was not ready. In Knoxville, Burnside bleated. In Washington, Halleck and the president fretted, and in Chattanooga, Grant fumed, "I have never felt such restlessness."

Then, on top of everything else, probably as a result of the movement of Johnson's and Cleburne's Divisions, came an unconfirmed report that Bragg was pulling out entirely, either retreating or going up to join Longstreet. Grant liked neither possibility. He had no need to wonder what the president would have to say to him if Bragg succeeded in the latter of those designs, and as for the former, Grant was loath to think of the Confederate general making off before receiving the little lesson in warfare that Grant had been at such pains to prepare for him. If Bragg was really leaving, Grant wanted to know about it, to stop him if possible, or at least to take advantage of him.

He needed to probe the Confederate lines, and so he ordered Thomas to advance a division toward the Confederate positions on the plain between the town and Missionary Ridge. Out of the midst of the undulating plain rose a 100-foot hill, standing almost alone. It was known locally as Orchard Knob, and it was a key point on the Confederates' advanced picket lines. Grant told Thomas to take it.

Around two o'clock on the afternoon of November 23, the divisions of the Army of the Cumberland began to marshal in front of their breastworks—not the one division Grant called for, but all four of the divisions that Thomas had available in this sector. Thomas might be nicknamed "Old Slow Trot," but he liked to do things up right. Twenty-three thousand men of the Army of the Cumberland, fully twice as many soldiers as had taken part in the famous Gettysburg assault known as Pickett's Charge, massed on the plain. First came the thin line of skirmishers, then the line of battle, shoulder to shoulder and two ranks deep. Behind them the file-closers—lieutenants and sergeants—took their positions, and several hundred yards to the rear another line, minus the skirmishers, duplicated the whole array. Near the center of each regiment's line of battle marched the color guard, sergeants and corporals of proven courage, the most honored members bearing the state and national flags. For a rarity, enough of the "field music" was on hand to drum the men forward. Here was the pomp and glory of war nearly every boy had imagined when he enlisted but that few of them had seen in their two years' experience of its hardships and horrors.

From all around the Chattanooga area, Union troops whose orders did not require them elsewhere scrambled for vantage points to see the show. From the Confederate gun line atop Missionary Ridge, from the main line of rifle pits at the base of the ridge, and from the advanced picket outposts like Orchard Knob, Southerners watched what they took to be a really gigantic Yankee troop review. Then throughout the Union formation a series of orders were shouted, echoed by a chorus of company officers; a bugle blared, the drums burst into a rolling, stuttering rattle, and the serried ranks stepped off at a steady marching pace like some immense painting of

Napoleon's legions sprung to life and striding right out of the canvas at the gaping Confederates. Brigadier General Thomas J. Wood, commanding one of the divisions in the assault, could not help admiring the grand spectacle their advance presented. "It scarcely ever falls to the lot of man," he wrote, "to witness so grand a military display."

The Confederates soon recovered from their amazement, readied their weapons, and as the formation came into range, opened fire. Still, no amount of artillery fire support from the ridge top was going to prevent a solid four-division battle line from taking the advanced picket outposts, and after a brief struggle around Orchard Knob, the surviving Southern pickets hurried back to the main Confederate lines as best they could. Thomas had used a great deal of force to accomplish his purpose, but there was no denying he had gotten the job done. From Grant shortly came word to hold the position that had been won. The Federal commander now had the information he wanted—Bragg was still in place—and the curtain had been raised on what was to be one of the most dramatic battles of the Civil War.

3
"THE DESIRED POINT"

Thomas's assault on Orchard Knob had told Bragg something as well. Clearly Grant was about to launch his offensive program. No time remained to carry out the right-flank strategy before the Union attack, and Bragg's choices now were simple: he could retreat toward Atlanta, admitting the failure of the whole six months' effort to hang on to Middle and East Tennessee, or he could prepare to fight a defensive battle in the positions he now held around Chattanooga. The choice was not as simple as it might have appeared, for Bragg did not like to fight defensive battles, avoided them whenever possible, indeed had never taken part in one since he was a captain commanding a battery of artillery in the Mexican War, and that was sixteen years before. Still, the alternative was unthinkable, so all that remained to Bragg was to practice an unfamiliar style of warfare and prepare to receive Grant's attack.

He took immediate steps to do so, sending orders to

Chickamauga Station for Cleburne and Johnson to abort their movement to Knoxville and get back to the main army post haste. He also issued an order to begin for the first time building breastworks along his gun line on the crest of Missionary Ridge so that it, rather than the line of rifle pits at the base of the ridge, could become the Confederate infantry's main line of resistance. If he was going to have to fight on the defensive, Bragg wanted the advantage of every bit of elevation he could get. Finally, impressed with the vulnerability of his right flank up on the far end of Missionary Ridge, he ordered his most experienced corps commander, Lieutenant General William J. "Old Reliable" Hardee, to come over from his position on the left and take command of the forces at the north end of the ridge, bringing one of his divisions, Major General W. H. T. Walker's, with him. The remaining troops of Hardee's Corps, still on the far left around Lookout Mountain, would now be commanded by his senior division commander, Carter Stevenson. The Confederate center, along Missionary Ridge, would be held by the corps of Major General John C. Breckinridge, while Hardee held the right with Walker, Cleburne, and Johnson.

Bragg's move to bring back Cleburne's and Johnson's Divisions came none too soon. Johnson and all but a single brigade of his division had already taken the train for Knoxville. For the immediate future they were beyond recall. Cleburne's Division and the odd brigade of Johnson's turned around and marched back to Missionary Ridge. They approached their designated position at the north end of the ridge around the middle of the afternoon on Tuesday, November 24, about twenty-four hours after the "grand military display" that had brought their recall orders. Once again they were not a moment too soon. Cleburne rode on ahead of his troops. As he and an officer of Hardee's staff surveyed the position assigned to him, a signalman dashed up to announce that blue-clad infantry in large numbers were even then surging up and over two detached hills just beyond the north end of the ridge. Cleburne meant to make those hills part of his position, and turning to bring up his lead brigade, three regiments of Texans, he ordered them to drive those Yankees off the nearer of the two hills and hold it themselves.

The Yankees, actually Midwesterners of the 47th Ohio, had other ideas. They tossed the Texans back off their hill and tried to follow up by taking the end of Missionary Ridge itself. This time it was the Texans' turn to dig in their heels and hold their ground. The two sides then settled down to snipe at each other across the deep, wooded ravine that separated the hill from the ridge. As his other two brigades came up, Cleburne quickly

WILLIAM J. HARDEE

Born Georgia 1815; Hardee was graduated from the U.S. Military Academy in 1838, twenty-sixth in his class of forty-five; commissioned into the 2d Dragoons, he served in Florida and was promoted to 1st lieutenant in 1839; he studied at the Royal Cavalry School at Saumur, France, returning to the U.S. in 1842; promoted to captain in 1844, he was captured early in the Mexican War but returned to duty and earned two brevets; afterward, he taught cavalry tactics at West Point and served on the frontier; his *Rifle and Light Infantry Tactics*, published in 1855, became the Army's standard training manual for years to come; also that year he was promoted to major in the newly formed 2d Cavalry Regiment, an elite unit that included Albert Sidney Johnston, Robert E. Lee, George Thomas, E. Kirby Smith, Earl Van Dorn, and John B. Hood among several other future Civil War generals; after service in Texas, Hardee became commandant of cadets at West Point; he was promoted to lieutenant colonel in 1860, but deployed them in strong positions to support the Texans. This end of Missionary Ridge, known as Tunnel Hill because the railroad tunnel passed through it a few yards south of where Cleburne's men were now deploying, offered definite possibilities as a defensive position. In preparing to use them, Cleburne demonstrated why he was the best division commander in the Army of Tennessee. All he and his furiously entrenching soldiers needed now was some time.

Across the way, a mile and a half or so beyond the line of Federal troops facing Tunnel Hill, Sherman decided that what his command needed right now was time—time to consolidate its gains and to prepare for a Confederate counterstroke he

resigned in January 1861 after Georgia's secession from the Union; he soon entered Confederate service as a colonel and was elevated to brigadier general in June 1861; after organizing troops in Arkansas, he led them to Kentucky; promoted to major general in October 1861, he commanded a corps at Shiloh the following April; thereafter most of his service was with the Army of Tennessee; promoted to lieutenant general in October 1862, he led his corps with great skill at Perryville, Murfreesboro, and Chattanooga, where his stand at Missionary Ridge helped save the army from total destruction; following General Braxton Bragg's removal in December 1863, Hardee temporarily headed the army but declined the permanent command; during the 1864 Atlanta Campaign, he openly resented Hood's promotion to command the Army, and performed inconsistently; after Atlanta's fall he was reassigned at his own request and commanded troops in opposition to General W.T. Sherman's March to the Sea and in the Carolinas; he surrendered with General J.E. Johnston in April 1865; after the war he settled at Selma, Alabama, where he engaged in planting and various other enterprises; he died at Wytheville, Virginia, in 1873. Known as "Old Reliable," General Hardee was among the Confederacy's most experienced and competent corps commanders; his inability to get along with Bragg and Hood, however, proved quite detrimental.

CARTER L. STEVENSON

Born Virginia 1817; Stevenson was graduated from the U.S. Military Academy in 1838, forty-second in his class of forty-five; commissioned a 2d lieutenant in the 5th Infantry, he was promoted to 1st lieutenant in 1840; he performed well during the Mexican War, and in 1847 was promoted to captain; after the war he served in Texas, against the Seminoles in Florida, and in the Utah Expedition of 1858; following the outbreak of the Civil War, he resigned his commission to offer his services to the Confederacy; commissioned colonel of the 53d Virginia Infantry, he was promoted to brigadier general in March 1862 and posted to the Department of East Tennessee; under the command of Major General E. Kirby Smith he commanded a division during the Kentucky Campaign; in October he was promoted to major general; ordered to Mississippi, Stevenson commanded a division in the defense of Vicksburg, fighting at Champion Hill and Big Black River; surrendered with the rest of the Vicksburg garrison in July 1863, he and his division were paroled but not exchanged; in a direct violation of his parole, Stevenson joined General Braxton Bragg's Army of Tennessee at Chattanooga, where he commanded one of the out-manned divisions driven from Lookout Mountain in November 1863 and joined in Bragg's retreat into Georgia; in 1864 he commanded a division in General John B. Hood's Corps during the Atlanta Campaign, temporarily heading the corps upon Hood's promotion to army command; Stevenson performed with mixed results during that campaign, at Nashville, and in the Carolina Campaign; paroled for the second time at Greensboro, North Carolina, in May 1865, he returned from the war to become a civil and mining engineer in his native Virginia; he died in Caroline County, Virginia, in 1888. Although he held important commands for most of the war and performed faithfully, General Stevenson proved to be largely ineffective as a field commander.

JOHN C. BRECKINRIDGE

Born Kentucky 1821; member of an old and honored Bluegrass family; attended Centre College, the College of New Jersey (now Princeton), and studied law at Transylvania University; practiced law briefly in Lexington in 1845; after a short residence in Iowa, he returned to Kentucky and married Mary Cyrene Birch; despite his family's Whig background, he took an interest in Democratic politics; saw no action during the War with Mexico, but visited Mexico City as major in the 3d Kentucky Volunteers; served in the Kentucky legislature from 1849 to 1851, and in the U.S. House of Representatives from 1851 to 1855; nominated and elected Vice President of the United States on the James Buchanan ticket in 1856, the youngest in American history; in 1859, a year and a half before his term was to expire, he was elected to the U.S. Senate by the Kentucky legislature; in 1860 accepted presidential nomination of the Southern Rights wing of the split Democratic Party; favored southern rights, and  when Kentucky declared for the Union in September 1861, he accepted a commission as Confederate brigadier general; in 1862 promoted to major general, commanded the reserve corps at Shiloh, defended Vicksburg, and failed in an attack on Baton Rouge, but fought desperately at Murfreesboro; in 1863 participated in General Joseph Johnston's Campaign to relieve Vicksburg; in 1864 commanded the Department of Southwest Virginia, and accompanied General Jubal Early in the raid on Washington; on February 4, 1865, President Davis appointed him secretary of war; following Confederate surrender, he escaped to Cuba, then to England, and finally to Canada; disclaimed all political ambitions, returned to Kentucky, and resumed his law practice. He died in Lexington, Kentucky, in 1875. "What a handsome and imposing appearance he made! Tall, straight, dignified, he was the ideal Kentuckian among Kentuckians," exclaimed a soldier. "Elegantly appareled, wearing the full dress uniform of a Confederate major-general, his bearing was indeed knightly. Boys, he'll do..., ain't he grand?" General Lee considered him a "lofty, pure, strong man...a great man."

felt was sure to follow. He sent orders for his men to halt and dig in.

The long-awaited Union movement had finally started. The wet weather that had plagued Sherman the past few days played one final trick by washing out the pontoon bridge at Brown's Ferry, leaving one of his four divisions stuck in Lookout Valley along with Hooker's troops. No matter; he would proceed with the three he had, and Grant arranged for him to borrow one from the Army of the Cumberland, supplied by way of the still functional pontoon bridge at Chattanooga.

The operation began shortly after midnight on the morning of November 24. On the north bank of the Tennessee (though actually at this point the river flows south, and the "north" bank is really the west bank), Sherman's men had brought up 116 pontoons for use as assault boats. Each would be manned by four oarsmen and would carry twenty-five assault troops. In careful silence Brigadier General Giles Smith's Brigade of the Fifteenth Corps loaded and shoved out into the river and proceeded with muffled oars. Officers had their men load their rifles but not perform the final step of the loading procedure, placing a percussion cap in a nipple on the weapon's hammer. That way no hotheaded soldier could give the game away by firing prematurely, but when the officers gave the word, every man could be ready to fire within a couple of seconds.

It was an eerie ride. One soldier remembered "darkness...so dense under the clouded sky and in the shadows of the forest-lined shore" that they could hardly see the next boat in line. "The Rebel picket fires on the opposite bank glimmered through the mist," he recalled. "We could see the guards throwing wood upon them, and once heard the challenge of a sentinel, but rarely was there any sound save the steady monotone of the river's rushing water."

Their target landing zone was a stretch of the south bank on either side of the mouth of Chickamauga Creek, about half a dozen miles upstream from the town of Chattanooga. Union

observers had carefully noted the positions of each
Confederate picket post, and now specially detailed officers
displayed lanterns on the north bank to signal the boats pre-
cisely where to start pulling for the opposite shore. The 8th
Missouri led the assault, angling toward the muddy bank just
above the mouth of Chickamauga Creek. The 55th Illinois
swept past in their wake and headed for the stretch just below
the creek's mouth, each boat aiming for its assigned picket
post. The Confederate sentinels suspected nothing until they
heard the Yankees splashing through the shallows. Then it was
too late, and one picket after another found himself surround-
ed and looking into the muzzles of two dozen Springfield rifles.
All but one of them decided to go quietly. The last one trig-
gered off a single shot "in his nervous surprise," as he apparently represented to his captors a few moments later. The
Confederate camps seemed to take no notice of the noise, and
Smith's men quickly and quietly rounded up the whole lot of
the gray-clad sentinels and sent them back to the north bank
as prisoners.

So far, so good. The rest of Smith's Brigade was soon
ashore, and the boat crews took their pontoons back to the
north bank to begin ferrying more troops across while Smith's
men began to construct a perimeter. The Confederates still
made no response, and by dawn two full divisions, about 8,000
men, were on the south bank. At first light, Sherman noted with
satisfaction that the murky weather was holding. A drizzling
rain, scudding wisps of fog, and a ragged cloud deck so low
that the crest of Missionary Ridge and upper two-thirds of
Lookout were invisible above it guaranteed just the sort of low-
visibility day he wanted for sneaking up on Bragg's right flank.

The engineers arrived at daybreak and took over the pontoons for bridging purposes—one long span, 1,350 feet,
across the Tennessee itself and another shorter one across the
mouth of Chickamauga Creek. They knew their business, and
Sherman thought he had "never seen any work done so quietly,

so well." A short while later, the small steamboat *Dunbar* came up the river from Chattanooga to aid in the ferrying operation. The bridge was completed shortly after noon, and by that time yet another division had been ferried over. Major General Oliver O. Howard, whose Eleventh Corps had been detached from Hooker's command and shifted into Chattanooga before the Brown's Ferry bridge broke, brought a brigade of his troops over from his corps's position on Thomas's right to reinforce Sherman still further and establish direct communication.

The morning's work had been almost a textbook-perfect military operation—fast, precise, and powerful. Sherman now had a large force, more than three divisions with another one already marching over the new bridge, positioned beyond Bragg's right flank. Visible through the mist just over a mile away from the new Federal bridgehead was the high ground at the north end of Missionary Ridge, their objective for the day. The rest should be simple—all Sherman's men would have to do was march over and get on the ridge, then roll southward right along the spine of it, sweeping Bragg's army to oblivion.

Somehow things did not quite work out that way. The preparations for the movement had been as complete as Sherman could have made them. He and his subordinates had gathered every bit of information they could get without giving up the secrecy of the operation. Naturally it would not do for Union officers to be running around the Chattanooga area, asking all and sundry for information about the geographical details of the country just beyond Bragg's right flank. Even if they could have been sure of getting reliable information from any of the local civilians (which was doubtful), they would have had to be just as certain that somebody would carry the news to Bragg, who would know just what it meant. Besides, the area's geography appeared plain enough. Anybody could see it right from the north bank of the Tennessee. Missionary Ridge was a landmark too massive to be missed or mistaken.

Or at least that was how it had looked from the north bank.

That was how it looked from the south bank too, as Sherman, at about 1:00 P.M., sent his powerful column marching off toward it across the intervening mile and a little more of undulating plain. Aside from some desultory skirmishing, the Federal troops encountered no Confederate resistance. They reached the high ground, and the blue-coated skirmishers went scrambling upward through the misty woods, panting clouds of white vapor in the cold, damp air and slipping on the thick layer of wet leaves underfoot. Up on the crest ahead, the only sentinels seemed to be the oaks and beeches with their shriveled brown leaves rustling in the breeze and the bare-limbed hickories and chestnuts. Reaching the top, they found it as deserted as it had looked from below, but something else they found surprised them. This hill was not quite part of the ridge. A long, deep swale separated it from another height just to the south.

The main line of battle came up the hill behind the skirmishers, and brigade commander Brigadier General Joseph A.J. Lightburn shared his skirmishers' perplexity at the vista it revealed. That other hill must be the true objective, he concluded, and ordered the 47th Ohio to go ahead and take it. They did so, just in time to meet the Texans from Cleburne's Division coming up the other side. With help from other Federal regiments, Lightburn's men beat back the Confederates but were in turn unable to drive them off of yet another height beyond. This hill too proved to be a detached part of the range, separated from the true Missionary Ridge by yet another deep saddle.

By now it was 3:30 P.M., and the sun, which had briefly broken through the day-long overcast, had once again vanished in the murk. Off to the southwest, the looming bulk of Lookout Mountain, briefly revealed by the brief break in the weather, was more deeply obscured than ever by bulging dark-gray clouds that promised more rain and an even earlier approach of darkness than would otherwise have come on this late

November afternoon. From his command post back near the mouth of Chickamauga Creek, Sherman followed the movements of his troops by means of a relay of signalmen, but this did not quite convey the subtleties of the complex terrain at the north end of Missionary Ridge. He later reported that by 3:30 on November 24 his men had "gained...the desired point." Thinking that his troops were actually astride the ridge itself, he concluded that Bragg would have to respond with a counterattack to get them off of there. That being the case, they had better make use of the last fleeting minutes of daylight to select defensive positions and begin to entrench them. He issued orders accordingly, and the pause was deeply appreciated by Cleburne, who, though he did not know its reason, did know that he needed time to prepare for the next Union advance.

If Sherman could have known the true situation his men faced that afternoon, including just how thin Cleburne's forces on Tunnel Hill were at this moment, he would undoubtedly have pushed on and actually taken the position astride the ridge that the whole day's operations were designed to secure. Even Cleburne would have been hard put to stop him, given Sherman's numerous tough, veteran troops. If the Federals had taken Tunnel Hill, Bragg's situation would have been just as desperate as Sherman thought it was, and perhaps he really would have launched that counterattack. Instead, Sherman blithely informed Grant that his men were on the high ground (true enough), almost to the tunnel (also true, for what it was worth), and ready roll up Bragg's line in the morning (a big mistake). In fact, it was the Confederates who still held the key position on the northern end of the battlefield, and Sherman's men were separated by a deep saddle and a great deal of bloodshed from "the desired point" he had in mind.

All that being the case, Bragg could have felt relatively satisfied with the day's action if not for simultaneous events at the opposite end of the Confederate line—on fog-shrouded Lookout Mountain.

4
"They Never Fought Better"

The rising waters of the Tennessee River that had broken the pontoon bridge at Brown's Ferry had done a big favor for Joe Hooker. By doing so they had stranded the fourth of Sherman's divisions, that of Brigadier General Peter Osterhaus, on the west side of Confederate-held Lookout Mountain, and that made for a change in Grant's battle plans that was very much to Hooker's liking.

Six months before, Hooker had stood at the pinnacle of his military career, as commander of the Army of the Potomac, the republic's largest. Then, however, he had met "Bobby Lee," on whom he had promised to have no mercy, and Stonewall Jackson, at a place called Chancellorsville, and nothing had ever been quite the same for "Fighting Joe" Hooker since. The assignment to command the Eleventh and Twelfth Corps detachment to Chattanooga offered a chance to redeem him-self. The problem was that Grant was not particularly enthusiastic about him as a general and had cast him for a bit part in the script for the coming Battle of Chattanooga. That definitely did not suit the erstwhile prima donna. Thomas was his imme-

JOSEPH HOOKER

Born Massachusetts 1814; graduated U.S. Military Academy 1837, twenty-ninth in his class of fifty cadets; brevetted 2d lieutenant assigned to artillery; on frontier duty, fought in Seminole wars, and held a staff assignment at West Point; served conspicuously in Mexican War, earning three brevets; captain 1848; resigned his commission 1853; engaged in farming in California and served as colonel in the state militia; offered his services to the Union at the outbreak of the Civil War but was initially snubbed owing to poor relations with General Winfield Scott; commissioned brigadier general U.S. Volunteers May 1861; led a division in the Peninsular Campaign and at Second Bull Run; major general U.S. Volunteers May 1862; commanded First Corps and was wounded at Antietam September 1862; promoted brigadier general U.S. Army to date from the battle; named to command the Army of the Potomac January 1863; routed by badly outnumbered Confederates at Chancellorsville, but received the thanks of Congress for his subsequent defense of Washington May 1863; relieved at his own request in June; sent West, took command of the newly formed Twentieth Corps Army of the Cumberland, which he led with great success at Chattanooga and during the Atlanta Campaign; resigned when overlooked for the command of the Army of the Tennessee following the death of General James B. McPherson; for the balance of the war he exercised various departmental commands; brevetted major general U.S. Army for Chattanooga victory; remained in the regular army until his retirement in 1868; died 1879. Although the disaster at Chancellorsville tainted his career, General Hooker proved to be a competent combat officer at division and corps level. While he hated his sobriquet "Fighting Joe," it was nonetheless appropriate.

PETER J. OSTERHAUS

Born Prussia 1823; Osterhaus received a military education in his native Prussia but, like so many others of his generation, he was forced to leave Europe after participation in the revolutions of 1848; he settled in the United States in the early 1850s, first in Illinois and then in St. Louis, where he found a home among that city's large German population; at the out-break of the Civil War he served the Union as major of a Missouri battalion, with which he participated in the capture of Camp Jackson and in the Battle of Wilson's Creek; commissioned colonel of the 12th Missouri Infantry, he commanded a division in the Battle of Pea Ridge in March 1862; promot-ed that August to brigadier general, he held numerous commands in the Trans-Mississippi; in January 1863 he moved east of the Mississippi to participate in the Vicksburg Campaign; he commanded a division in the Army of the Tennessee and was wounded in the fighting at Big Black River Bridge; continuing with the Army of Tennessee, he performed admirably during the Chattanooga Campaign; during the Atlanta Campaign of 1864, Osterhaus was frequently absent from his com-mand but nonetheless garnered a promotion to major general of volunteers; he periodically directed the Fifteenth Corps in General William  T. Sherman's March to the Sea but, in January 1865, was transferred to the Military Division of West Mississippi and served as chief of staff to General E.R.S. Canby during the Mobile Campaign; mustered out of volunteer ser-vice in January 1866, he was U.S. consul at Lyons, France, from 1866 to 1877, while maintaining a residence and business in St.Louis; he later served as deputy consul at Mannheim, Germany, from 1898-1900; placed on the army's retired list as a brigadier general by act of Congress in 1905, General Osterhaus died at Duisburg, Germany, in 1917, only weeks before the U.S. declared war on the general's homeland.

diate superior, and through him he appealed to Grant. Reluctantly, Grant allowed that if it proved impossible to get that bridge repaired and move Osterhaus along to join up with Sherman, then Hooker could go ahead with a much more ambitious version of the script. He would have three divisions in that case—Brigadier General John Geary's of his own Twelfth Corps, Osterhaus's of Sherman's Fifteenth Corps, and Brigadier General Charles Cruft's of Thomas's Fourteenth Corps. Letting all three divisions sit idle on the west side of Lookout Mountain made no tactical sense at all. If they could not be brought around by way of the bridge, then Hooker could take them and attack the only Confederate target accessible from his position, the lines on towering, 1,400-foot Lookout Mountain itself. Perhaps, as Grant reasoned, he could at least distract Bragg from the real show—Sherman's attack up at the other end of the line.

A joke had been making the rounds in the Federal camps to the effect that "one of these fine mornings, Joe Hooker is going to take Lookout Mountain." It really did seem like a laughing matter—the prospect of any body of troops, no matter how aggressive their commander, trying to take that immense rock-crested piece of land away from determined defenders—but Joe Hooker was about to try. November 24 was not a fine morning at all. Rain dripped monotonously and low clouds and fog as often as not obscured the mountain itself from viewers below even as they hid Sherman's landing on the other side of Chattanooga. The men in the ranks found the prospect definitely not funny anymore. A soldier of the 149th New York recalled being ordered to fall in "with one day's rations, blankets, and sixty rounds of ammunition, to make an attack upon Lookout Mountain." The news came as quite a shock. "The men had not breakfasted," he recalled, "and this announcement took away their appetites." Peering upward through the murk for a glimpse of the craggy summit they had viewed in clearer weather, some of the men nervously asked each other, "Does the general expect us to fly?"

Hooker's plans called for purely pedestrian movements, but the tense soldiers could be forgiven their disbelief. Lookout Mountain is itself a long ridge that extends—northeast to southwest—from Tennessee all the way through Georgia and into Alabama. It is highest at its northern terminus, or point, where it towers over the town of Chattanooga. Its heavily wooded slopes rise steeply from the banks of the Tennessee River's Moccasin Bend. About two-thirds of the way to the top, the slope moderates, forming a sort of shoulder, or bench, on which, in 1863, a few houses and a couple of small farms perched. From the shoulder, the slope once again becomes more abrupt until it reaches the base of the palisades, a more or less sheer rock face by which the mountain rises the last fifty feet or so to its summit, the point. The palisades extend clear around the point and for miles and miles along both sides of the mountaintop, which is itself a plateau that spreads to a width of two or three miles from its narrow tip at the point.

The Confederate defenders, two brigades of Major General Benjamin F. Cheatham's Division since the detachment of Longstreet to East Tennessee, had quite properly drawn their defensive line along the lower edge of the bench, where they could, theoretically at least, command all of the slope below that point. Their advanced picket line ran along the bank of Lookout Creek, west of the mountain, then curved around the north end of the mountain to the banks of the Tennessee and back along the lower slopes to Chattanooga Creek, on the east side of the mountain. On top of the mountain, there were more Confederates, two brigades of Stevenson's Division, whose primary mission was to guard against any possible Union attempt to reach the top by using one of several possible gaps in the palisades over a stretch of some ten miles to the southwest of the point. Stevenson's men were also expected to support two batteries of artillery, one of them long-range Parrot guns, which had for weeks been trying their luck at shelling the Federals in Chattanooga, without much success.

On the whole, four brigades to cover something as large as Lookout Mountain was spreading the defense rather thin. Much of the thinning out, as well as an all-around command shuffle, had come within the previous twenty-four hours. In reaction to the assault on Orchard Knob, Bragg had moved Walker's three-brigade division out of Chattanooga Valley, between Lookout Mountain and Missionary Ridge, and around to the north end of the ridge, just south of Cleburne's position. To plug the gap this left in his line, he had taken one brigade from Stevenson's Division and one from Cheatham's, which was temporarily under the command of Brigadier General John K.

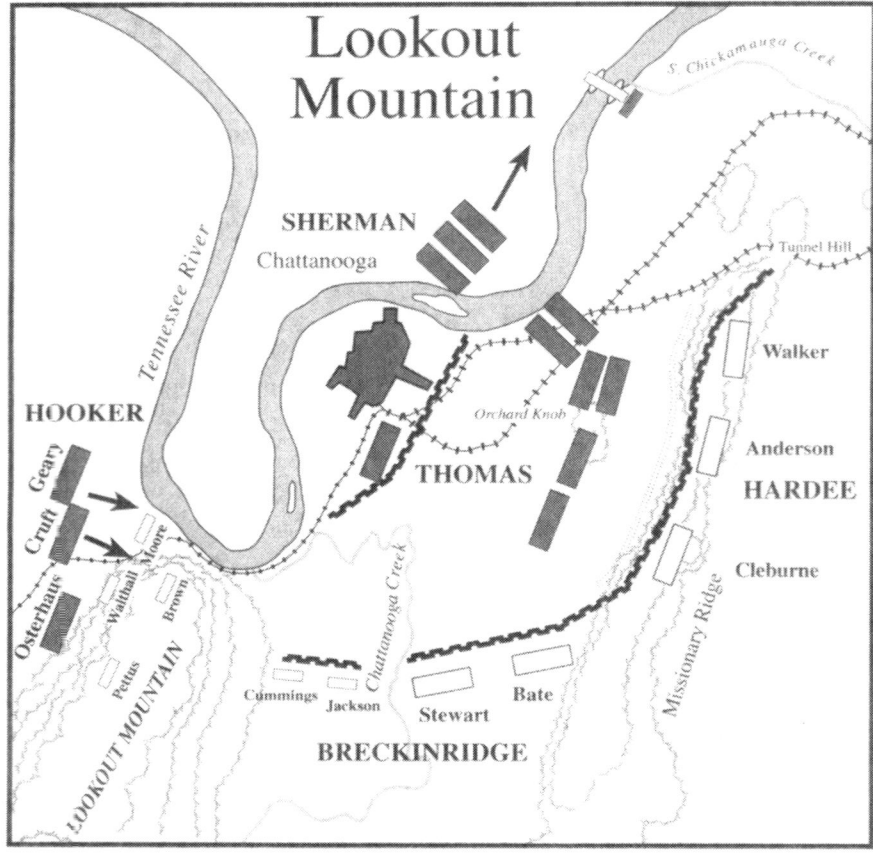

JOHN K. JACKSON

Born Georgia 1828; graduated with honors from South Carolina College in 1846, Jackson passed the bar in Georgia and started a law practice in Augusta; he served in the local militia—the Oglethorpe Infantry—and was elected captain, then lieutenant colonel; in May 1861, following Georgia's secession from the Union, he became colonel of the 5th Georgia Infantry and was assigned a post on the white sand beaches of Pensacola, Florida; there he saw action on Santa Rosa Island and developed a friendship with his commander, General Braxton Bragg; in January 1862 he was promoted to brigadier general and ordered to Grand Junction, Tennessee, to organize troops for the coming campaign; he commanded a brigade under General Bragg at Shiloh and performed credibly; later in 1862, he participated in Bragg's Kentucky Campaign; temporarily assigned to Lieutenant General Leonidas Polk's command at Murfreesboro, Jackson protested Polk's ill-advised order to attack a Federal stronghold and after three bloody assaults he fell back, losing some 300 men; during 1863 he was assigned to guard Bragg's communications at Bridgeport, Alabama; his brigade was heavily engaged at Chickamauga in September 1863, as one of his regiments lost some sixty-one percent—the second highest percentage of losses in the battle; at Chattanooga in November 1863, Jackson held temporary command of one of the divisions charged with the defense of Lookout Mountain, where he apparently showed little initiative as his overstretched command was driven from its positions; his brigade, though, performed well in covering Bragg's retreat into northern Georgia that followed the Federal assault on Missionary Ridge; Jackson commanded his brigade in the early stages of the Atlanta Campaign, but in July he was sent to Savannah, where he participated in the unsuccessful defense of the city; he served in the Carolinas for the remainder of the war; after the war he returned to Augusta to resume his law practice, but in February of 1866, while on a trip to Milledgville, he contracted pneumonia and died. Like many a Confederate general, Jackson lost credibility at Chattanooga, but he served faithfully throughout the war and at times showed true ability.

Jackson, while Cheatham was absent on leave. Nor was Jackson the only officer commanding at a higher level than usual. Since Hardee, who commanded the corps to which these units belonged, had been sent around to the right the evening before, Stevenson now exercised overall command on this end of the front, while Brigadier General John C. Brown commanded his division. Several of the officers had not even had time to view by daylight the sectors they now commanded. Hooker thus had at least a few factors working for him in undertaking to storm the seemingly impregnable mountain.

The west slope of Lookout Mountain was held by Brigadier General Edward C. Walthall's Mississippi Brigade. Walthall ranged one of his three regiments along the front facing Lookout Creek to the west. Another he angled back on his left flank, stretching (at least theoretically) all the way back to the base of the palisades. Each was spread so thin that half its numbers were required just to man a decent picket line. The main line, naturally, amounted to little more than a picket line with some log and stone breastworks. The third brigade Walthall held in reserve. Yankee movements in the valley out front sounded suspicious that night, so the Mississippians were up, armed, and in line before dawn. Daylight brought dense fog and dim glimpses of Union troops—no one could say how many—marching upstream along the far creek bank, toward the Confederate left. By 9:00 A.M. the fog had lifted to a level about halfway up the mountain. Walthall's men could see a large Federal formation moving toward their advanced picket line along Lookout Creek, and a lively firefight flared up almost immediately.

Walthall thought his men were doing well and figured he could hold on if he could just get some Confederate guns to deliver counterbattery fire on the Union artillery that was punishing his command from the high ground on the far side of Lookout Creek. Then things began to go wrong. The Federals hit his left like an avalanche—and they were moving not up the mountain but rather sideways along the slope. The Confederate line there did not, as it turned out, reach quite to the palisades, and the Union line most definitely did. Flanked and outnumbered, Walthall's left collapsed.

Things had been working out just the way Hooker had planned. While Osterhaus's Division, reinforced with one of Cruft's two large brigades, had applied head-on pressure to the Confederate line, Geary's Division, reinforced by Cruft's other brigade—glimpsed dimly through the fog by the Confederates—had swung upstream beyond the Rebel flank and then uphill and finally along the hillside heading back north to strike the crushing blow that had folded up Walthall's Mississippians. The single regiment on Walthall's flank— deployed as it had been in two skirmish lines with exposed left flanks—had had no chance against Geary's four brigades.

With his position going to pieces, Walthall became flustered and began to make mistakes, first declining to retire his brigade to the prepared position on the north end of the mountain where the Confederates had planned to make a stand, then committing his reserves piecemeal as individual skirmish lines. With considerable frustration, Walthall kept sending to ask his superiors when he was going to get some artillery support, when some more infantry, but his position was disintegrating too fast for anyone to have done much for him anyway. The Mississippians fought with desperate valor. Lieutenant Colonel A.J. Jones thought his 27th Mississippi "never fought better." But no skirmish line, no matter how fiercely defended, was going to stop Geary's exultant Federals. The longer the Confederates resisted, the poorer their chances of escaping capture when the blue-coats swept around their flanks.

The Union troops were all but drunk on the exhilarating sensation of victory, and it made them feel as if nothing could stop them. For these soldiers of the Army of the Potomac, who had spent their war thus far following the likes of Hooker or less capable commanders in going up against Robert E. Lee, it was a new and heady draught. One of them spoke of their "joy" at finding they had turned the Rebel flank, while another likened their advance to "the rush of an avalanche." They exhibited their euphoria in the ferocity of their attacks. Brigadier General John C. Moore, whose Confederate brigade moved up to support Walthall's, noted of his Union attackers. "I have never before seen them fight with such daring and desperation," while Geary himself primly noted, "The men were full of animation and enthusiasm."

Walthall's regiment facing the creek was in desperate straits. The only trail going up from where they were zigged far south along the western slope before it zagged back toward the north end of the mountain. Geary's men had the southern switchback as soon as the left-flank regiment collapsed, leaving the men on Walthall's right to clamber uphill over logs and boulders and through ravines with Osterhaus's men right behind them and Geary's closing in along the slope from the south. Most of them did not make it, adding to the Union's rapidly growing catch of prisoners. As Geary's Division swung around the north end of the mountain and Osterhaus's moved up into line beside it, they swept up most of Moore's pickets as well.

Perched on the shoulder at the north end of the mountain was the farm of Robert Cravens. Since it marked the northernmost spine of the mountain running down from the point to the river, the Confederates had planned to make a stand there. A couple of cannon were in place, some rifle pits had been dug, and the buildings and stone fences of the farm provided as good a rallying point as the Southerners were likely to find. Moore's Brigade moved up and came into position on the Confederate right, its line running down-slope from the Craven's House, and Walthall and his officers tried to rally their men around the guns. This was the place to stop Hooker's relentless attackers, who by now must nearly have exhausted both their energy and their ammunition.

The storming of Orchard Knob twenty-four hours earlier

had been witnessed by tens of thousands, but this battle on
the mountainside was being fought behind a curtain of fog. In
the Confederate rifle pits along the base of Missionary Ridge
and in the Union lines in front of them, at Grant's new command post on Orchard Knob itself, and at Bragg's headquarters
atop Missionary Ridge, men of both sides had listened all
morning and into the afternoon to the boom of Hooker's
artillery, the rattle of musketry, and the faint shouts drifting
down through the mist from the mountain. After noon, the
flash of rifle fire on the north slope of Lookout told that the
battle had moved back to the prepared Confederate position
around the Cravens House. Captain J.W. Wright, a young
Confederate staff officer in front of Missionary Ridge, could not
understand how the Federals could be sustaining such an
attack against a position that had appeared "so nearly impregnable that earth-works there seemed almost unnecessary."
Surely the Yankees could not take that mountain. Then, as if on
cue, the cloudy curtain parted and swept back to reveal the
scene of battle to the thousands watching below. "Suddenly, as
a cloud rolled away," Wright recalled, "we saw our line of
breastworks swarming with men for nearly half a mile and
flags waving there."

"What flag is that?" gasped several anxious onlookers.

Someone nearby had a field glass, and a hush fell as he
briefly scanned the mountainside. "There, it is plain enough,"
he finally spoke. "It is the stars and stripes."

Presently more flags appeared over the victorious battle
line, and the Confederates had no need of field glasses to
know the bad news about their identity. The Army of the
Cumberland's positions were closer to the mountain, and from
the Federal lines cheer after cheer went up. Bands struck up
"Yankee Doodle" or "Hail Columbia," artillerymen fired
impromptu salutes with shotted guns aimed at Missionary
Ridge, and infantrymen tossed their hats into the air and
yelled themselves hoarse.

The stand at the Cravens House had never had a chance. Federals advancing along the base of the palisades charged around its uphill flank. In the center, in the yard of the Cravens House, Confederate artillerists could not bring their guns into action because their field of fire was blocked by the fugitive remnants of Walthall's Brigade. Close on their heels came Geary's bluecoats, clambering and scrambling over logs, boulders, and rough terrain on sheer adrenaline, yelling wildly all the while. The battery's horses had been sent to the rear and could not be brought up in time, so the gunners had no choice but to abandon their pieces and join the flight. Moore's Brigade tried to stem the tide, but with Walthall's Brigade broken, Moore's was forced to fall back as well.

Hooker's men swept past the Cravens House, rounded the north end of the mountain, and began to work their way back southward along the east side. After about another quarter mile of retreat, the Confederates were finally able to stabilize their line. Stevenson, who had found that neither his riflemen nor his cannoneers could do more than nuisance damage to the Union formations advancing below the sheer rock face on which they sat, sent half of one of his two brigades down from the summit, and it spelled Walthall enough for him to regroup and refill his survivors' cartridge boxes. With his brigade back in line, the Confederates were able to extend their position all the way to the foot of the palisades, cutting off one of the Federals' favorite methods of flanking every position they had previously tried to hold. Finally, the weather came to the Southerners' rescue. The brief window of clear weather passed; more and heavier fog moved in, and the misting rain resumed. It was late afternoon by this time anyway, and Hooker finally called his weary but elated troops to a halt, though firing continued along the lines for hours.

Bragg was disgusted with the performance of his troops on Lookout Mountain and not very happy with Stevenson's and Jackson's roles in presiding over the debacle. In truth, neither had turned in an inspired performance, but both had probably done about as well as most officers would have in that situation. Everyone had tended to think of the mountain as an impregnable fortress, and the Union attack and its success had caught them all by surprise. The defenders were too few, and because movement on the mountain was so difficult, once Hooker's men got the advantage of position on them, there was little they could do but flee.

Despite his disgust, Bragg really had not invested much in the holding of Lookout Mountain. Unlike the north end of Missionary Ridge, it did not cover his own line of supply, and ever since the opening of the Cracker Line, it did not cover the enemy's either. Some of his officers had even thought he contemplated abandoning it without a fight, and he had certainly—and correctly—given its defense a much lower priority than that of Missionary Ridge. By late afternoon on November 24, about the time Hooker was calling a halt to his advance, Bragg sent orders for his troops to evacuate such portions of Lookout Mountain as they still held, along with their positions in Chattanooga Valley. Everyone would be moving back to Missionary Ridge after nightfall. Stevenson's and Cheatham's Divisions (Cheatham had at about this very hour returned from his leave) would march along the ridge up to the north end, where they would come into line next to Walker's and Cleburne's Divisions, thus reuniting Hardee's Corps.

Down on Orchard Knob, a satisfied Ulysses S. Grant wrote dispatches informing Washington of the day's success. Hooker had carried Lookout Mountain, and Sherman had won, as he supposed, a position astride the north end of Missionary Ridge. Tomorrow, if Bragg was still here, Grant would finish the business.

5

"LIKE THEY WERE GOING TO WALK RIGHT OVER US"

The skies cleared after dark that night, and a bright full moon lit the great natural amphitheater in which the last two days of battle had been fought. Along the crest, slopes, and base of Missionary Ridge the Confederate campfires flickered, while Union fires shone from Sherman's positions near the north end of the ridge, through the outskirts of Chattanooga, to the base of Lookout Mountain. No campfires lit the mountainside—too close to the enemy—and it was a cold, damp bivouac for the exhausted troops there. Instead, through most of the night as the Confederates carried out their evacuation, the rifle flashes of firing between the rival skirmishers looked to one observer down on the plain like "twinkling sparks upon the mountainside," and to several others like "myriads of fire flies on the mountain side."

It was very cold that night, and one soldier recalled that "thousands of sleepless men lay shivering on the ground" or, when they could, crowded around campfires, boiling coffee. They were treated to an unusual spectacle, a nearly complete lunar eclipse. Many of the men thought this sign in the heavens must be an omen of something, though interpretations varied with the state of mind of the interpreter. It seemed safe to say, even without the moon, that there would probably be a battle the next day and someone was going to lose.

Just after midnight, as the firing on Lookout Mountain began to subside and things began to settle down around Union headquarters, Grant sat down to write out his orders for the next day's action. Hooker could continue his little sideshow off on the Union right, starting at dawn and making sure that all the Confederates were off of Lookout Mountain. Once he completed that chore, he should march down the mountain, across Chattanooga Valley, and on to Missionary Ridge. He should strike the ridge at Rossville Gap, just across the Georgia line and presumably beyond Bragg's left flank. Once he got there he could turn and roll up Bragg's line on the ridge the way he had the line on the mountain the day before, though Grant figured such a maneuver would be unnecessary by that time. The main event in the next day's program Grant planned for Sherman. Thinking his friend and most trusted subordinate was already astride the ridge and Bragg's right flank, he meant for the red-bearded general to roll up Bragg's line from that end first thing in the morning, destroying the Confederates' position and probably cutting or at least pinching their line of retreat at the same time, since the railroad back to Atlanta, along which Bragg would have to withdraw, ran right through the tunnel in Tunnel Hill. Thomas would pile in with his Army of the Cumberland as soon as Sherman got things rolling, and Hooker's activities would be all but irrelevant.

Across the way at Bragg's Missionary Ridge headquarters, the Confederate high command had already met to discuss the question of whether they should even remain in place to await whatever additional miseries Grant might have planned for them on the morrow. With Bragg were Hardee, Breckinridge, and a number of division and brigade commanders. Cleburne was not at the meeting but assumed that after the debacle on Lookout Mountain, Bragg would be inclined to cut his losses and get away while the getting was good. Of the officers who spoke up at the meeting, Hardee was for retreating. Breckinridge was against it. If they could not stop the Yankees in these mountains, he argued, where could they stop them? That was a good point. Besides, the Kentuckian and former U.S. vice president had his fighting blood up. "I never felt more like fighting than when I saw those people shelling my troops off of Lookout today," he confided to a staff officer, "and I mean to get even." Bragg himself was probably not inclined to retreat since it would mean the final abandonment of any hopes of reaping a victory from the Confederacy's major effort to reinforce his front. Both he and the South had too much invested in the struggle for the gateway city of the southeast to walk away from it now.

November 25 dawned bright, clear, and cold. It was greeted with new waves of cheering from the Union troops in the plain, who spied the Stars and Stripes floating at the rocky point of Lookout Mountain. Early that morning Hooker's men on the mountain had gotten the idea of putting it there. A couple of parties had set out to scale the palisades, and on reaching the top, they found it deserted. The flag was planted, and Hooker had already—through the eagerness of his troops—accomplished the first of his objectives for the day.

Sherman was not finding matters nearly so favorable up at the other end of the Confederate line. The terrain, of course, was not as he had envisioned, and that being the case, Sherman was having a very hard time figuring out just what it was instead. As a result, his action that morning was tentative and halting. It was eleven o'clock before he actually launched a real attack against Cleburne's positions on Tunnel Hill, and Cleburne appreciated every bit of the delay for perfecting his preparations and receiving reinforcements. Sherman's first assault was carried out by Brigadier General John M. Corse's Brigade. Like all of Sherman's troops, these Ohioans, Illinoisans, and Iowans were veterans of Vicksburg and many another hard-fought battle, and believed nothing could stop them. They were almost right.

Corse, with just under 1,000 men, attacked head-on at the north end of the ridge, where it was defended by a slightly larger number of Texans in Brigadier General James A. Smith's

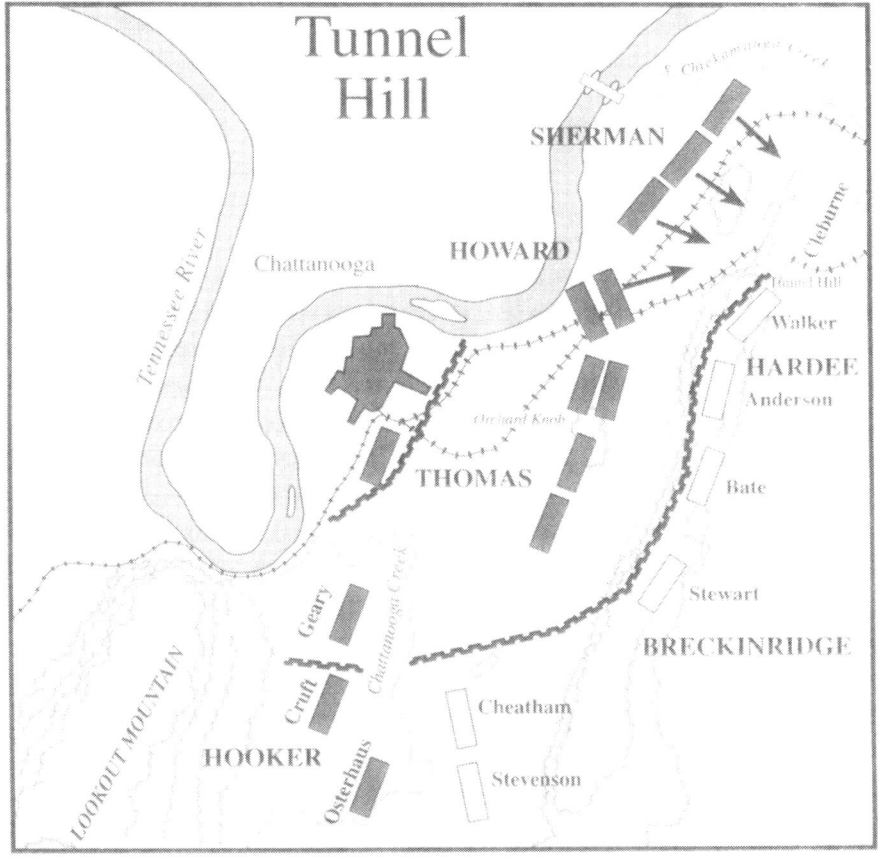

Brigade of Cleburne's Division. The charging Midwesterners were "in easy canister and musket range" from the very moment they crested their own hill and started down the swale that separated them from the end of the ridge. Corse believed in leading from the front, and he was doing so very literally, charging along in the front line of his advancing brigade, urging the men on. They did not seem to need much urging. From the rear line, Colonel Charles C. Walcutt of the 46th Ohio thought the "terrific fire" was so intense "it seemed almost impossible for any troops to withstand it, but," he added, "so eager were the men to take the new position that they charged through it, all with a fearlessness and determination that was astonishing." Across the bottom of the ravine they went and up the slope toward the Rebel position, crouching low, rifles at the ready, in open skirmish order. "This was business," thought a Confederate officer up on the hilltop, and Corse's soldiers had the air of men who knew their business. To the watching Texans, the bluecoats looked "like they were going to walk right over us."

Still, they were only flesh and blood and sadly susceptible to the rifle bullets of the Confederate infantry and the artillery's canister—a whole bucket of lead slugs rammed down the mouth of a cannon. When fired it produced an effect something like a gigantic sawed-off shotgun. The four twelve-pounder guns of Swett's Mississippi Battery grew red-hot with firing it. Corse went down badly wounded, and his men were driven part way back down into the swale while a chorus of Texas yells rose from the exultant defenders. Their yells caught in their throats, though, when almost immediately they saw Corse's men coming on again, Walcutt leading this time. Again the air just below the crest seemed full of flying lead. "The fire we was under was terrible," wrote an Ohioan, "Everything seemed to be flying but the Rebels, and they was busy shooting at the Yanks." But the Yanks were firing back now in what was becoming a shoot-out with rifles at fifty yards. "We could see what we were doing," one of the Texans recalled, "When we killed a man, we knew it. We saw him fall. Two Yanks achieved to get killed but a few yards from our breastwork." Rebels were getting killed too, as the Federals concentrated their fire on the exposed gunners of Swett's Battery. The Confederates had the breastworks, though, and that advantage finally began to tell.

As Walcutt's men began to fall back down the slope, still firing, Smith's Texans, sensing the release from the nervous tension of the vicious short-range firefight, spontaneously surged over their breastworks in pursuit, screeching their Rebel yells. The Federals, however, were in no mood to be hurried. Blazing away from the shelter of rocks, logs, tree trunks, or just the damp, leaf-covered earth, they "punished the enemy good," as Walcutt proudly recalled, and "sent him running to his works." Smith and a good many of his men were down, including one of his colonels. Command of the considerably thinned out Texas Brigade passed to Colonel Hiram Granbury, who had to stretch his scant manpower still further by detailing a number of his infantrymen to stack their rifles and help man the guns of Swett's Battery in place of the fallen cannoneers. The battery by now was commanded by a corporal, the senior gunner still on his feet.

Within half an hour, Walcutt's men came on yet again, but again the Texans stopped them. Thereafter, Granbury's and Walcutt's men continued to pop away at each other with a lively skirmish fire for the rest of the day, but for the moment they had pretty well established that Walcutt's Midwesterners would stay about halfway down the slope and Granbury's Texans would stay behind their breastworks.

Sherman was frustrated. This was not at all the sort of thing he had promised Grant. It was now about noon, and he was supposed to be well on his way to winning the battle rather than contemplating, from a range of only a couple of hundred yards, this first Rebel-held hill that he simply did not seem able to take. His advance was being stalled by a terrain feature that according to all of his preliminary reconnaissance was not even supposed to exist. Now he intended to find out just how the land lay in front of him, and so he sat on the back of his large horse on the top of the hill from which Corse had launched his attack and studied the nearby Confederate position despite warnings from the prone soldiers nearby that this ground was swept by enemy rifle and canister fire. He would stay until he was satisfied he had seen all there was to see, and so he did, somehow avoiding injury or death.

What he saw was that the north end of Tunnel Hill (or Missionary Ridge) was a very difficult place to attack. Walcutt's men could have given him a more detailed exposition of that point. The question was what to do about it, and Sherman had three possible choices. He could shift his attack to the northwest face, over on the Chattanooga side, or he could shift it to the northeast face, the reverse slope, or he could bring up reinforcements and try again right here. He had plenty of unused troops available; after all, fifteen of his sixteen brigades had yet to see action on this day. In the end, though, his decision would have to be very much of a guess, since he really could not know the details of the two other possible approaches. He knew this one was bad, so he opted for the northwest face, probably reasoning that it would be easier to bring up reinforcements to that point.

He guessed wrong. The northwest face turned out to be the worst of the three possibilities. Cleburne had feared that Sherman might go after the northeast face, about which he felt some concern. Another attack on the north end would at least have made use of the damage Walcutt's men had already inflicted on the Texans and Swett's Battery, whose position Cleburne considered "the weak point of Smith's [now Granbury's] line." By contrast, the northwest face was the easiest place for the Confederates to receive an attack.

The new assaults started at about 1:00 P.M. This time

Sherman managed to get four more of his brigades engaged, though not in a coordinated fashion. Somehow things just did not seem to work right for the Ohio general on this day. Cleburne, by contrast, was having one of his best days of the war, deftly shifting troops from one position to another within his compact hilltop position and aiming—and often himself leading—well-timed limited counterattacks to shift the tide of battle when the attackers seemed to be gaining ground. Once again Sherman's men fought bravely. The 93rd Illinois charged to within twenty paces of the Confederate breastworks near the western mouth of the tunnel. Its colonel, Holden Putnam, somehow got his horse up that steep incline, and there he was, conspicuously urging his men on, sword in one hand and regimental colors in the other, until a Rebel bullet found him and he toppled from the saddle dead. His men held on though, crouching in the leaves and exchanging fire with the Confederates in the breastworks. Beside them fought the 27th Pennsylvania of Howard's Eleventh Corps, which was also part of Sherman's command for this operation. The 27th's commander, Major P. A. McAloon, was wounded three times but refused to allow himself to be carried from the field until his regiment retired after hours under enemy fire. Both regiments, as well as a number of others that clung stubbornly to the slope, fired away the whole contents of their cartridge boxes, and the men were rummaging the cartridge boxes of their fallen comrades before the fight was over. A farmer named Glass had been unfortunate enough to build his house, barn, and outbuildings at the foot of the ridge near the mouth of the tunnel, and they now became key tactical strongpoints, much sought after by both sides. Fighting swirled furiously around them, and they changed hands repeatedly until Confederates on one of their forays from the ridgetop set fire to them. The billowing sheets of flame and clouds of dark gray smoke gave a lurid touch to a battlefield scene in which the low-hanging sulfurous white clouds of powder smoke had replaced the previous day's natural fog. Under bright, cold sunshine the thick white smoke drifted downhill and off toward Chickamauga Creek, while the heat of the flames drove the dark smoke from the Glass farm buildings up into a column above the low-hanging banks of gunsmoke.

By the time the end came, the sun had dropped more than half way down the western sky toward Lookout Mountain and it was about three o'clock in the afternoon (in this war, no two participants' watches ever seemed to keep the same time). The tenacious Federals clinging to the slopes were making life miserable for Cleburne and his men, inflicting casualties and sometimes driving the gunners away from their pieces. Cleburne described their fire as "one continuous sheet of hissing, flying lead," that pinned down the Confederate troops on that stretch of his line. Worse yet, one of Cleburne's regimental commanders reported to him that he thought the unshakable tenacity of the attackers was gradually disheartening the Confederate defenders.

Consulting with his officers, the Irish Confederate decided it was time to drive those men off the slopes for good and all. The Yankees had to be tired and almost out of ammunition. A little shove now might bring complete collapse and put a decisive end to the day's fighting. Cleburne ordered a bayonet charge to dislodge the Federals still clinging to the slope. Remarkably, they had more fight left in them than Cleburne had calculated and drove back his charge. Still the Confederate division commander believed he could break them and tried again. Again he was driven back, but a third charge proved as decisive as he had hoped. Some of the Confederates managed to flank their foes by descending the ridge through a ravine near the tunnel. Their appearance on the flank of troops who were indeed exhausted and without much ammunition, and belonged to decimated formations, brought the pressure on the Federals to the collapse point. So great was the shock of the Union troops at finding the Confederates emerging from the ravine near the tunnel that many of them actually thought the Rebels must have snuck down the back slope and come through the tunnel to surprise them. Actually that would not have worked, and, as events demonstrated, nothing like it was necessary. Cleburne collected a couple of hundred prisoners, and the other Yankees went streaming back down the ridge. No one who saw them had any doubts that Sherman's attacks on Tunnel Hill were over for the day.

6
"THIS GRAND SPECTACLE"

One of those who saw them was Grant, watching in growing dismay from his prime vantage point on Orchard Knob. He had not been having a very good day so far. First there had been Sherman's delay. Then when Sherman's attack finally did get started in earnest, it had seemed to go nowhere. Obviously, Sherman was not on Missionary Ridge, and no one needed to mention that there had been a serious mistake about topography. On top of everything else, Hooker's movement toward Rossville Gap, from which Grant had actually been expecting no significant results, seemed to be fulfilling his expectations.

That it was so was not really Hooker's fault. He had gotten his troops moving at a good hour, after making sure that the top of Lookout Mountain was indeed free of Confederates. Down the mountain his column had swung at a good pace and then on across gently rolling Chattanooga Valley. Then, as seemed to be the way of things in this campaign, complications had arisen just one mile from his goal. This particular complication took the form of Chattanooga Creek, a deep and fast-flowing stream that had been made even more so of late by the incessant rains. As the Confederates had retreated across the valley the night before, they had very thoughtfully destroyed the bridge behind them, and now Hooker was at a loss to get his command across. Finally some resourceful Missourians of Osterhaus's Division rigged up a makeshift foot bridge capable of crossing one man at a time, providing the man in question had a good deal of nerve. Hooker's engineers worked on a better model while the infantry made its way across, and finally Hooker decided to take the infantry and go on, leaving the artillery to catch up whenever it could get across the creek. By that time, however, it was 3:30 P.M. and some three hours had been lost in making the crossing.

Grant had learned of Hooker's problem early in the after-noon. Now he had witnessed Sherman's repulse at Tunnel Hill. Along with these battlefield setbacks, he also had the assur-ance that the authorities in Washington were getting more and more impatient about the situation in Knoxville, where Burnside was still semi-besieged by Longstreet. In response to Grant's up-beat telegram of the evening before, Lincoln had sent congratulations and a reminder: "Remember Burnside." Halleck had plainly stated that he did not think Burnside was going to be able to hold out much longer unless Grant did something about the situation. Clearly, Grant's superiors expected decisive action here at Chattanooga as a prelude to a march to relieve Burnside, and they expected that decisive action to begin at once. It was just as clear to Grant, as he watched Sherman's men scrambling back down the slopes of Tunnel Hill with Cleburne's Confederates in hot pursuit, that nothing decisive was likely to happen today unless he came up with a new idea or two.

Throughout the day Grant and the others on Orchard Knob had been watching as Stevenson's and Cheatham's Divisions marched along the crest of Missionary Ridge on the way to take position beside Cleburne at the north end. Grant interpreted that to mean that Bragg was responding to Sherman's pressure by massively reinforcing that front. In fact, this was not strictly so. Bragg had already made a series of decisions over the past two days to hold that end of his line in greater strength, and that was natural since the Confederate line of supply and retreat ran off in that direction to the railroad and the bridges over Chickamauga Creek. On the other hand, Cleburne with only a minor assist from neighboring troops had handily repulsed Sherman's attack, and Bragg felt no special need to shore up the defenses there as a result.

Nevertheless by mid-afternoon, even before the final

THOMAS J. WOOD

Born Kentucky 1823; Wood was graduated from the U.S. Military Academy in 1845, fifth in his class of forty-one; originally assigned to topographical engineers, he served as a 2d lieutenant in the Mexican War, earning a brevet for Buena Vista; after transferring to the dragoons he saw a variety of duties on the frontier, during the Kansas border wars, and on the Mormon Expedition, achieving the rank of captain, 1st Cavalry, in 1855; in 1861, as Southern officers left the Army in large numbers, Wood rose rapidly through the ranks, becoming major in March, lieutenant colonel in May, and colonel, 2d Cavalry, in November; he had in the meantime been commissioned into the volunteer army as brigadier general in October; he commanded a division in General Don Carlos Buell's Army of the Ohio at Shiloh, in the advance on Corinth, and at Perryville; wounded at Stone's River on the last day of 1862, Wood refused to leave the field until the day's fighting had ended; he returned to lead repulse of Sherman's Tunnel-Hill assaults, Grant thought that perhaps it might help Sherman if he could apply a little pressure elsewhere in order to distract the Confederates from the Tunnel Hill sector. Since Hooker was still stuck at the crossing of Chattanooga Creek, Grant's only option for creating a diversion was to have Thomas either do something or at least pretend to do something with his Army of the Cumberland against the center of the Confederate line along Missionary Ridge. The order Grant had written out the night before had spoken of having Thomas's men possibly "carry the rifle-pits and ridge directly in front of them," but the idea then had been to do so only after Sherman had started rolling up the Confederate line. That definitely had not happened yet, but Grant began to think

his division in the Tullahoma Campaign and at Chickamauga in September 1863, where his prompt execution of an order nearly resulted in the destruction of the Army of the Cumberland; on directions from General William Rosecrans, Wood pulled his division out of line to fill a gap that did not exist thereby creating an actual gap through which the Rebels poured only moments later; Rosecrans lost his job, but Wood was not disciplined and, two months later at Chattanooga, his troops were among those who spontaneously charged up Missionary Ridge, routing the Confederates; Wood led a division with conspicuous skill throughout the Atlanta Campaign and was wounded on September 2 at Lovejoy Station, again refusing to leave the field; returning to duty he led his division at Franklin and directed the Fourth Corps at Nashville; in February 1865 Wood received the well-deserved promotion to major general, U.S. Volunteers; brevetted through major general, U.S. Army, he reverted to his regular rank of colonel; he served in Reconstruction Mississippi until 1868 when he was retired for disability due to wounds with the rank of major general; in 1875 he was permanently retired as brigadier general, U.S. Army; a member of the U.S. Military Academy's Board of Visitors, General Wood remained active in veterans' organizations until his death at Dayton, Ohio, in 1906.

that perhaps it was time to move to the next stage of his plan anyway.

Thomas, along with most of the other high brass of the Army of the Cumberland, was also on Orchard Knob at the time. The 100-foot hill seemed to be an observation point too fine to be passed up. Indeed, a battery of Union artillery was even posted on the hill and was dueling with Confederate guns on the ridge. Grant stood and thought for a while and then discussed the matter casually with Brigadier General Thomas J. Wood, a West Point classmate and now the commander of one of Thomas's divisions that would have to carry out any possible movement against the ridge. Wood thought they might be able to accomplish something and said he would be glad to try if Grant gave the order. More and more convinced that this was

GORDON GRANGER

Born New York 1822; Granger was graduated from the U.S. Military Academy in 1845 thirty-fifth in his class of fifty-one; originally posted to infantry, he won two brevets during the Mexican War, after which he served on the frontier with the U.S. Mounted Rifles; promoted to 1st lieutenant in 1852, he remained in that grade until the onset of the Civil War; promoted to captain in May 1861 (in August the Mounted Rifles was redesignated the 3rd U.S. Cavalry); during this period he also served briefly as a volunteer lieutenant colonel on the staff of General George B. McClellan in western Virginia; moving to the Western Theater, Granger worked on Samuel Sturgis's staff at Wilson's Creek, Missouri, in August 1861, after which he was appointed colonel 2d Michigan Cavalry; promoted to brigadier general in March 1862, he commanded the thing to do, Grant decided to find out what Thomas thought about the matter. The large, stolid, and slow-moving comman-der of the Army of the Cumberland had previously stated that he did not want his men to try storming the ridge. The position was too strong, and his troops would be slaughtered. Perhaps, though, Thomas would see that the situation warranted some risk-taking. In his quiet, unassuming way, Grant sauntered over to where Thomas was standing, avidly surveying the ridge through his field glass. Might it not be time for the Army of the Cumberland to take a hand and go ahead and start its advance against the ridge, Grant asked in his normal mild tone of voice. No one wrote down what, if anything, Thomas said in reply. At any rate he never lowered his field glass, continuing to scan the ridge the whole time. Grant was a patient man. He

the Cavalry Division, Army of the Mississippi, at New Madrid, Island No. 10, and in the advance on Corinth, Mississippi; in July he assumed command of an infantry division and in September was promoted to major general, U.S. Volunteers; from November 1862 through January 1863, Granger headed the District of Central Kentucky and, thereafter, the Army of Kentucky; in June 1863 he took command of the Reserve Corps, Army of the Cumberland, with which he played a major role in the September 1863 Battle of Chickamauga; there, fol-lowing the collapse of the Federal army, Granger, on his own initiative, rushed the Reserve Corps to the relief of General George Thomas, helping to save the Army of the Cumberland from possible destruction; Granger then commanded the Fourth Corps, Army of the Cumberland, at Chattanooga and at Knoxville; after a leave of absence, during which he missed the Atlanta Campaign, Granger assumed command of the District of South Alabama; in the closing stages of the war he directed the Thirteenth Corps in the Department of the Gulf, participating in the capture of Forts Gaines and Morgan and, ultimately, Mobile; brevetted through major general, U.S. Army, he continued in the regular army as colonel of the 15th Infantry; plagued by recurring poor health, General Granger died on active duty at Santa Fe, New Mexico Territory, in 1876.

took this piece of rudeness in stride and walked quietly back over to where he had been standing along with his staff.

And that was the situation as Grant witnessed things going downhill—both literally and figuratively—for Sherman. Patient Grant might be, but he had his limits. While the Union battle plan went to pieces around them, Thomas placidly observed and rejected any suggestion of getting involved himself, while his corps commander on this sector, Major General Gordon Granger of the Fourth Corps, seemed to have nothing better to do than to pretend to be a captain of artillery and personally direct the fire of the hilltop battery. By three o'clock Grant had seen enough. Dropping his mild manner, he barked out an order like an army group commander on the field of battle, which is what he was. "General Thomas, order Granger to turn that battery over to its proper commander and take command of his own corps. And now order your troops to advance and take the enemy's first line of rifle pits."

By that, Grant meant Thomas was to initiate the program mentioned in his orders of the night before to "carry the rifle-pits and ridge." Taking the rifle pits was the first step, and Grant intended that the troops should catch their breath and regroup after taking them before pushing on up the ridge. Staying at the rifle pits would have been an absurdity, since they were obviously situated right under the guns of the Confederates on the ridge. Somehow Grant's intention did not get transmitted to the officers who were to lead the attack. Perhaps Thomas honestly misunderstood Grant; perhaps, being irritated by Grant's order and by having to take any orders at all from Grant, Thomas did not want to understand Grant.

In any case, when the signal guns were fired forty minutes later and the Army of the Cumberland advanced, their officers had very garbled ideas of what they were supposed to be doing. Over in the Fourteenth Corps sector, many officers understood that they were to push on immediately for the crest of the ridge, while the two Fourth Corps division commanders involved in the assault, Wood and Major General Philip Sheridan, had a much different impression. Wood thought the order was definitely to stop at the rifle pits. Sheridan realized as his men were forming up for the attack that he did not know where he was to stop. He sent an aide galloping off to find out, but the young officer had not yet returned when the signal came to advance. Other officers at various levels thought the order was simply to advance against the enemy, without any specified stopping point.

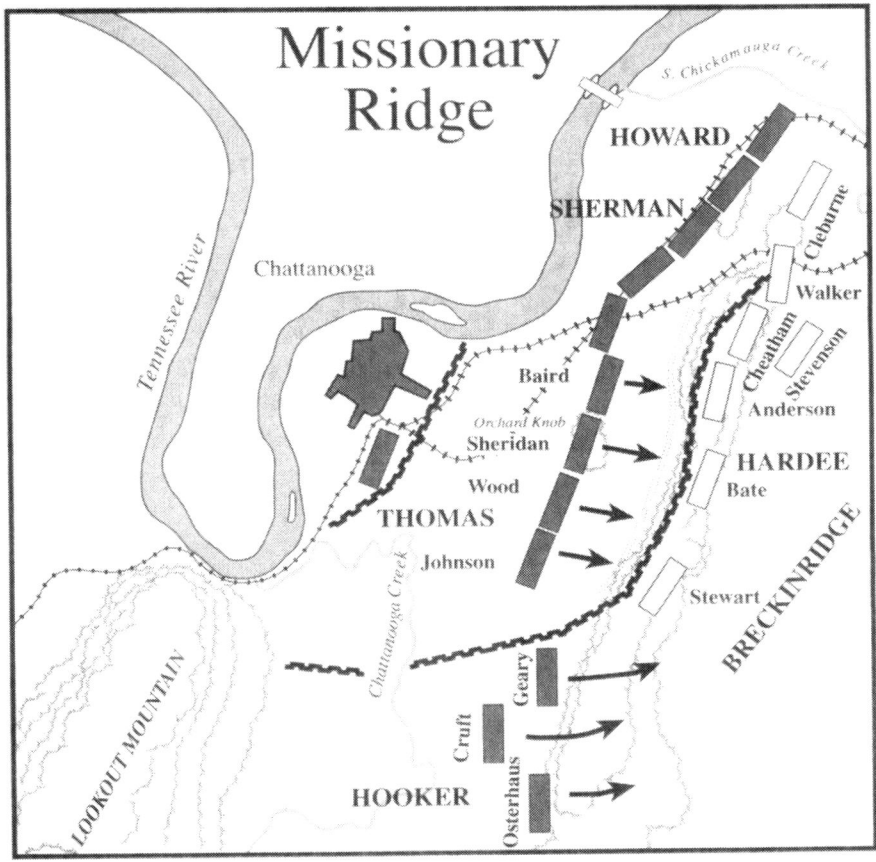

PHILIP HENRY SHERIDAN

Born New York 1831; Sheridan's date and place of birth remain matters of speculation; Sheridan himself gave conflicting information; he may have been born in Ireland or aboard ship during his Irish parents' passage to the United States; whatever the case, the family moved to Ohio when Sheridan was still an infant; he entered the U.S. Military Academy with the class of 1852, but disciplinary problems delayed his graduation by a year; he finished thirty-fourth in the 1853 class of fifty-two that included John Bell Hood, James B. McPherson, and John M. Schofield; after years of service on the frontier with the 4th Infantry, Sheridan was still a 2d lieutenant on the eve of the Civil War; promoted to 1st lieutenant in March 1861 and captain, 13th Infantry, in May, he served as chief quartermaster and commissary for the Army of Southwest Missouri and was detailed to General Henry Halleck's headquarters during the advance on Corinth, Mississippi; in May 1862 he entered the volunteer army as colonel of the 2d Michigan Cavalry and, by July, was promoted to brigadier general, U.S. Volunteers; he commanded an infantry division at Perryville and Stone's River, gaining promotion to major general, U.S. Volunteers, to date from December 1862; Sheridan's division was routed at Chickamauga in September 1863, but spearheaded the unauthorized assault that drove the Confederates from Missionary Ridge in November; when General Ulysses S. Grant was named overall commander of Union forces and went east to face General Robert E. Lee, he selected Sheridan to lead the Army of the Potomac's Cavalry Corps; throughout the spring and early summer of 1864, Sheridan's troopers duelled with the once-supreme Rebel cavalry with mixed results; he was victorious in the clash at Yellow Tavern, in which Confederate cavalry commander J.E. B. Stuart was mortally wounded; in response to Confederate General Jubal Early's move on Washington, Grant created the Middle Military Division and placed Sheridan in command; Sheridan's Army of the Shenandoah, consisting of two infantry corps and three large divisions of cavalry, defeated Early at Winchester and Fisher's Hill but narrowly escaped disaster at Cedar Creek when the Rebels surprised Sheridan's army during his absence; Sheridan's ride from Winchester to Cedar Creek to rally his men is among the most well-publicized events of the war; during the fall and winter of 1864-1865, in an awesome display of total war, Sheridan's troops laid waste to the Shenadoah Valley, depriving Lee of much-needed supplies and incurring the wrath of Southerners for generations to come; the fiery Sheridan became a national hero; having been promoted to brigadier general in the regular army in September 1864, he became major general in November; in the spring of 1865 Sheridan, with the bulk of his command, rejoined Grant on the Petersburg front and played a pivotal role in the closing stages of the war; given wide discretion, Sheridan's cavalry ran roughshod over the Rebels at Five Forks and Sayler's Creek, finally cornering Lee's army near Appomattox; while extremely successful on the battlefield, Sheridan's abrasive manner and quick temper led to the unfair removal of General G.K. Warren, a controversy that raged for years; immediately after Lee's surrender, Sheridan was dispatched to the south Texas border with Mexico to discourage French intentions in that country; thereafter his heavy-handed conduct as the reconstruction commander of the Fifth Military District (Texas and Louisiana) brought his removal; when Grant became president and William T. Sherman filled his spot as commanding general, Sheridan became lieutenant general; as commander of the Military Division of the Missouri, he was an aggressive prosecutor of the Indian Wars; during this period he was also an official observer of the Franco-Prussian War and supported the creation of Yellowstone National Park; in 1884, on the retirement of Sherman, Sheridan became commanding general; in June 1888 he was awarded his fourth star; General Sheridan died shortly thereafter at Nonquitt, Massachusetts. He remains among the most influential soldiers in the nation's history.

WILLIAM B. BATE

Born Tennessee 1826; Bate attended the Rural Academy in Sumner County until his father's death in 1842, when he left home to work on a steamboat that transported goods between Nashville and New Orleans; he participated in the Mexican War and was elected lieutenant of the 3d Tennessee Infantry; upon his return from the war, he started a Democratic newspaper in Gallatin; after a term in the Tennessee legislature, he studied law at  Lebanon (Cumberland University), and was a presidential elector in 1860; with the approach of the Civil War, he helped to organize Walker's Legion, which evolved into the 2d Tennessee Infantry; he enlisted as a private but was soon elected captain of Company I and later colonel; during the Battle of Shiloh in 1862, he was wounded in the leg and sidelined for ten months; for his heroism he was promoted to brigadier general in October 1862; returning to duty, he again performed conspicuously in the Tullahoma Campaign and at Chickamauga in September 1863; that November he took charge of the rear guard during General Braxton Bragg's desperate retreat from Chattanooga; earlier that year he had been nominated for the governorship of Tennessee, but he declined to stand for election, saying that he could never except civil honors while Union soldiers remained in Tennessee—he would continue to fight; promoted to major general in March 1864, he commanded a division throughout the Atlanta Campaign, in General John B. Hood's invasion of Tennessee, and in the Carolina Campaign, suffering two more wounds; paroled at Greensboro, North Carolina, in May 1865, he returned to Tennessee to practice law; he served as a Democratic presidential elector in 1876 and was elected governor of Tennessee in 1882 and 1884; in 1886 he was sent to the U.S. Senate, serving until his death at Washington, D.C., in 1905. General Bate fought vigorously as a soldier and proved just as determined as a politician in working to end Reconstruction policies in his state.

The reluctance of their commander, Thomas, and the confusion in the minds of many of their officers was not visible in the steady, solid ranks of the Army of the Cumberland. As they had two days before when they had stormed Orchard Knob, the Cumberlanders presented a magnificent spectacle, spread in parade-ground formations across the broad plain at the foot of Missionary Ridge. Once again thousands of eyes watched, and the soldiers themselves, as they formed their ranks, were aware of the incredible event of which they were a part. A lieutenant of the 64th Ohio recalled, "Far and near could be heard the bugle notes and the voices of the officers calling the men to attention, and as they sprang to their feet there was a great rustling of dead leaves and a snapping of dried twigs. I cast a hurried look to the right and the left, and on either hand, as far as I could see, stood two lines of blue coats with beautiful flags waving and bright arms gleaming in the pleasant afternoon sunshine. It was a splendid sight that sent the blood tingling to the finger tips." He figured the Confederates could see them too and wondered if it produced any effect on them. "We were standing in a stretch of open timber, but the leaves were all off the trees, and we were in plain sight. As we advanced, every Confederate soldier along the crest of the ridge in our front could take in our entire array with one sweeping glance."

He was right. The Confederates on the ridge had the best vantage points, and they were impressed. "Every movement in the plains below was visible to us," wrote the 20th Tennessee's Colonel James Cooper, "and a sublime scene was presented to our view, when the massive columns began their onward march." To Brigadier General William B. Bate, the 23,000 marching men on the plain below looked "like a huge serpent uncoiling his massive folds." Brigadier General Arthur Manigault was impressed with the technical skill of the great Union formation. "The sight was grand and imposing in the extreme," he wrote, "and I was much struck by the order and regularity of their movements, the ease with which they preserved their line, and the completeness of all arrangements. Such a sight I never saw either before or after, and I trust under the same circumstances never to see again." Private soldiers had similar reactions, a Floridian recalling, "We looked out on the plain, and with the precision of a dress parade their magnificent army came in view." With awe he noted the "superbly dressed" mounted officers, the bands playing, the "most wonderful array of splendidly equipped soldiers I ever saw," and "the old flag" that "waved beautifully at the head of each regiment."

Like Manigault, many Confederates found the vast martial array not entirely a reassuring thing to have aimed in their direction. "I think . . . I noticed some nervousness amongst my men," he wrote, "as they beheld this grand military spectacle, and heard remarks which showed that some uneasiness existed amongst them." The Federals out on the plain looked remarkably numerous. Manigault himself overestimated their numbers by a factor of two, while a soldier in an Alabama regiment recalled, "There was Grant's army, formed and forming in battle array, at least eighty thousand men in the valley below, in full view. It was a most uncommon sight even to veteran soldiers."

His count was off by a round 57,000 men, but he was right about the last point. These veterans of two years of warfare in woods, thickets, and rolling country had been in battle on several occasions but had rarely if ever seen more than a brigade or perhaps a division of their own or the enemy's troops ranged in open view on the battlefield. The sight appeared to have shaken many of them. To left and right along the relatively level, undulating ridgeline they could see only a few hundred of their comrades, while before them was spread a seemingly immense host. The impact of the view was expressed with humorous hyperbole by a Confederate in explaining his hasty flight from the battle. He was prepared, he maintained, to go up against two-to-one odds, "but when he heard old Grant command 'Attention World! By Nations right and left wheel,' he thought it was about time for him to retire."

Still these men were veteran troops who had often proved their willingness to fight and fight hard. Their position seemed like a strong one, and officers such as Manigault, who thought they knew a military impossibility when they saw it, "felt no fear for the result."

Thomas's men had approximately three-quarters of a mile to go to reach the line of rifle pits at the base of the ridge. Roughly the first half of this—more in some places, less in others—would be through an open woodland, the rest across an open field of cotton stubble. The bugles blared, the officers shouted their orders, and the bands struck up their patriotic tunes to the rhythm of 23,000 pairs of brogans crunching down alternately in the dry leaves of the forest floor. First came a heavy line of skirmishers, then, a couple of hundred yards to the rear, the main line of battle, shoulder to shoulder, two ranks deep. Another 300 or 400 yards to the rear came the brigades of the second battle line, closed up in columns the width of a two-company front for ease of movement, but ready to deploy into line when needed. The leafless woods provided no cover from the eyes of Confederate gunners on the ridge, and soon dozens of guns were blasting away as fast as their crews could ram home the new loads. The Union batteries thundered back, trying to beat down the Confederate fire. Out on the plain the Cumberlanders found themselves marching through an arching dome of ear-splitting, throbbing sound. A few men were hit, but the Federals soon discovered that the barrage was relatively ineffective despite all the noise, fire, and smoke it made. The Rebel gunners, unaccustomed to firing on such a steep downhill pitch, were aiming a bit high, at least at the outset.

As the Cumberlanders emerged from the woods they caught sight of the Confederate rifle pits and raised a great cheer. Almost immediately, however, they came under a much more intense fire. They were now just 400 or 500 yards out, and the Rebel infantrymen could go to work with their rifles, while the distance to the artillery was approaching the point-blank range at which hits were almost guaranteed. Up and down the line, Union officers ordered their men to the double-quick, and the pace of the charge picked up. In the rear line, companies and then regiments wheeled into line as the brigades deployed out from column into line of battle and then plunged onward over the cotton stubble in the wake of the first line. As they got closer to the rifle pits, the leading regiments accelerated from a trot to a run to an all-out sprint. True to their orders, they did not fire but rushed ahead with their bayonets. Up ahead, Rebels suddenly quit firing their rifles, groping in cartridge boxes, or fumbling with ramrods, and scrambled out of their trenches and up the steep slope of the ridge behind in desperate flight. Others decided not to risk it and threw down their guns in surrender. No sooner had Thomas's men steeled themselves for the final rush than the fight at the base of the ridge was over and the rifle pits were theirs.

For the Confederates, things had begun to go terribly wrong. In fact, the basic defensive scheme had been all wrong to begin with. The inexperience of Bragg and his generals in conducting defensive battles manifested itself in a very poor tactical deployment. With the troops divided between the rifle pits at the bottom of the ridge and the new breastworks at the top, the result was at each location a formation that was too thick for a skirmish line and too thin for a line of battle. The troops down in the rifle pits seemed to have been a bit confused about what they were supposed to accomplish there in case of enemy attack—for the understandable reason that their generals were not quite sure either. Some of the troops had orders to fire a volley and then flee up the ridge. Others believed that their mission was to resist in the rifle pits as long as possible. As the Yankees approached, those who thought it their duty to flee did so. Those who knew nothing of any such orders were appalled to see whole regiments decamping for the rear at virtually the first fire and became demoralized, surrendering or fleeing themselves, usually to fight no more that day. Others refused flight or surrender. From atop the ridge an anguished Manigault "could see some of our brave fellows fighting to the last, firing into the enemy's faces, and at last fall, overpowered by numbers."

One way or another, Confederate resistance in the rifle pits was quickly extinguished, and the troops there were lost to the defense of the ridge. Even those soldiers who on orders or on their own judgment planned to continue the fight once they got to the top of the ridge often proved to be of little further use. After climbing a steep, 600-foot slope at fear-induced speeds with the enemy or his bullets, at least, in hot pursuit, most of them could do little more than collapse on the ground, quivering, panting, and retching.

The question for the Federals was what to do now. In some units there was no uncertainty. As soon as the men had caught their breath, their officers ordered them on up the slope. In others the officers thought they were intended to remain in the rifle pits and tried to keep the men there despite the fact that they were now exposed to a more deadly fire than they had been during practically the entire charge up to that point. Some of Sheridan's troops actually got part way up the ridge before their officers heard that they were supposed to have stopped in the rifle pits below. Incredibly, the officers sent the men back down the slope, and only after they reached the bottom did they learn that the orders did indeed call for an ascent and that everyone else was already on his way up. Turning around, the panting soldiers retraced their steps, charging the ridge a second time. In still other units, officers saw the necessity of getting out of their present position and sent their men uphill on their own responsibility, while in still others the men themselves reportedly took the decision out of their officers' hands and charged for the crest. "It was evident to every one that to stay in this position would be certain destruction and final defeat," wrote Brigadier General August Willich. "Every soldier felt the necessity of saving the day and the campaign by conquering, and every one saw instinctively that the only place of safety was in the enemy's works on the crest of the ridge."

Up the slope went the Cumberlanders. Their officers found they had little to do in leading the troops, and that was just as well since they had all they could do just to keep up. The whole thing seemed almost impossible, even to the men who were doing it. "There never was such a bold or daring charge made or witnessed by the Army of the Cumberland," thought one of their officers. In this war assaulting forces had been butchered in front of far less formidable positions than this one. Yet somehow the Federals were pushing higher and higher up this incredible slope, and though they were taking casualties, their attack was not being broken up, as all Civil War experience said it should have been.

Partially this was because of the undermanned condition of the Confederate breastworks on the crest. Partially it was because fleeing Confederates from the rifle pits were blocking the fields of fire of their comrades on top of the ridge. And partially it was because Missionary Ridge itself, as Sherman could have told the Confederate defenders here, could be a very deceptive piece of terrain. From a distance it appeared to be a continuous and more or less smooth slope, but in reality its sides undulated in varying degrees of steepness even as they were rutted with dozens of large, deep ravines that sloped and wound up toward the summit and could provide a covered approach for whole regiments of attackers. If a defender used this complex terrain wisely, as Cleburne did up at the Tunnel Hill end of the ridge, it could reward him well. On the other hand, generals who assumed that the ridge's very size would stop attackers were in for some surprises. One of the worst of these was that the slope included large and numerous areas of "dead ground," dips in the earth where attackers could shelter, rest, or even advance without being exposed to the defenders' fire. Finally, along with everything else, the Confederates had drawn their line on top of the ridge contrary to good principles of military engineering. Instead of being at the military crest of the ridge—the point near the top at which the slope begins to diminish and a defender's field of fire covers most of the ground in front of him—it was drawn at the geographic crest— the very highest point of the ridge. That meant that just a few yards in front of the Confederate lines the Yankees could enjoy an enormous zone of dead ground, sheltered by the swell of the ridge as its slope grew more gradual toward the crest.

The men of the Army of the Cumberland shed their parade-ground formations as they started up the ridge. As the 24th Wisconsin's Major Carl von Baumbach put it, "After advancing beyond the first line [of rifle pits], the line of battle was not regular. The men took advantage of all obstacles in the way for shelter." Using every bit of cover they could find, the Cumberlanders worked their way laboriously up the ridge, pausing when necessary to regain their breath. To an observer back on Orchard Knob, they looked like migrating birds as their formations dissolved and reformed, bunching in covered areas and spreading out for dashes across ground swept by Confederate fire. Most often their groups took the shape of a "V" with the apex pointed uphill. The colors, a regimental officer or two, and some of the stronger men would be at the apex, while the rest of the regimental line—if such it could be called—trailed back to either side.

Afterward, no one could really say for certain which unit had first breached the Confederate line at the crest. Many claimed that honor, but in reality the attackers seem to have pierced the line in at least half a dozen places at once. Often the attackers would pause just below the crest to catch their breath and gather their strength before the final rush. Just as often, the Confederate defenders of that sector did not even realize that Yankees were lurking sometimes as little as ten or fifteen yards away and ten or twenty feet below. Then the Federals would surge over the crest and into the Confederate breastworks and gun emplacements before the defenders could react. A vicious struggle with rifles, bayonets, artillery rammers, and handspikes was soon over. The Confederates surrendered or made off down the back side of the ridge as best they could, while the Yankees fanned out in either direction to take other defenders in flank.

Troops of Wood's Division in the brigades of Willich and Brigadier General William B. Hazen were among the first Federals on top of the ridge and, indeed, had as good a claim as any to the coveted honor of being first. As they neared the top, Corporal Adam Preston took the colors from the hands of a badly wounded comrade. He was the sixth member of the 35th Illinois's color guard to take up the flag during the charge, the others, a sergeant and four corporals, having fallen wounded. The flag itself had now collected some thirty bullet holes. Twenty yards short of the Confederate breastworks the attack faltered. No dead ground was available at this point, only increasing numbers of dead men as several regiments jumbled together but hesitated to go on. Preston was hit and killed instantly. The 35th's commander, Lieutenant Colonel William P. Chandler, seized the colors and calling on the men to follow him, dashed toward the works. The crowd of blue-clad soldiers surged forward. A member of the 68th Indiana jumped over the breastwork and was shot dead. Chandler was over next, flag in hand, and a moment later the works were swarming with Federals. Everyone seemed to go over at once—including Lieutenant Matthew McInerny with the colors of the 86th Indiana and Sergeant Alfred P. Short with those of the 68th.

Perhaps a minute or two before, Lieutenant Colonel Bassett Langdon of the 1st Ohio had led another mixed command of strong-lunged soldiers from several regiments toward a battery a couple of hundred yards to the south. He made for a steep pitch that gave plenty of dead ground just below the crest. With fifty yards to go he called to his men to fix bayonets, and they did so on the run, while the commanders of the 41st Ohio and 23rd Kentucky echoed the cry to their men. Langdon halted the advance in the dead ground until several hundred men had come up and massed there. Then as he rose to give the order that would send them over the top, a Confederate bullet slammed into his face, and he toppled forward.

"I am not killed yet!" he growled to his stunned men. Not only was he still alive, but he had also seen the location of the Rebel that had gotten him. Several of them were firing from behind a log a few yards off to one side, thus allowing them to hit Langdon despite the steep slope behind which he and his men were sheltering. He ordered a detail of his troops to fire on the log and pin down the snipers. Then he gave the order, and the rest of his force clambered over the lip of the ridgetop yelling like fiends, while Langdon stumbled off to find a surgeon.

The Confederate battery on that particular protruding spur of the ridge was located only three yards from the edge of the slope. Suddenly the Yankees poured in on them, led by Major Joab Stafford carrying the colors of the 1st Ohio. He was the sixth man to do so since they had started up the ridge, and he was already bleeding from a leg wound. The fight for the battery was over in seconds. The 23rd Kentucky's Lieutenant Colonel James C. Foy, who had been standing next to Langdon when he was hit, was almost beyond taking prisoners. "Some of the rebels who had been murdering our men to the last moment," he wrote in disgust, "rolled over on their backs and looked up in a very pitiful attitude"—offering a surrender Foy was loath to accept. No time to bayonet them now anyway—let them surrender and find their way to the rear. Foy and his men swept on.

Elsewhere on the crest the story was much the same. When the 24th Wisconsin's color-bearer collapsed of sheer exhaustion, the regimental adjutant, Lieutenant Arthur MacArthur, grasped the flagstaff and, dashing out in front of the men, led them over the Confederate breastworks shouting, "On Wisconsin!" The eighteen-year-old lieutenant not only survived the charge and the war, but went on to father a son, Douglas, who would play an even more prominent role in America's future wars.

The tough frontiersmen of the 2d Minnesota led Colonel Ferdinand Van Derveer's Brigade up the ridge. One of the hardest-fighting brigades in the army and among the heroes of the Battle of Chickamauga, Van Derveer's Brigade pushed toward a battery of Rebel guns on a prominent spur of the ridge. Confederate fire dropped six of the seven members of the 2d's color guard, a shell cut the flagstaff in two, and another tore the blue field and white stars out of the flag. Still the last member of the color guard carried what was left of the banner upward, and the regiment followed as best they could. The protruding finger of high ground on which the Confederate guns perched gave them a deadly enfilade fire on Federals moving up the slope for hundreds of yards in either direction, but it also made them vulnerable. The sides of the spur were exceptionally steep, and under them clustered Van Derveer's men, unknown to the Confederate gunners. As elsewhere on the ridge, a brief pause preceded a wild rush, and the Federals swept over the battery even as the gunners were in the process of loading another round. Those artillerists who could do so fled, leaving rammers still in the tubes. The Minnesotans claimed two of the pieces and the 35th Ohio three more.

Only in the immediate vicinity of Bragg's headquarters did the situation on the ridge initially show any promise at all for the Confederates. There, Bate's Division appeared to have beaten off the attack against its lines. Bragg was riding the line, congratulating the troops, when he realized that the

Federals had broken through further to the right and ordered Bate to pull some of his troops out of line and clear the ridge in that direction. In fact, the situation there was much worse than Bragg or Bate realized. Though Bate was a good officer and his men good soldiers, the chief reason their lines had not broken was that they were facing Sheridan's Division, where confusion about orders had led to the assault on the ridge being started, then recalled, and then started again. As Bate prepared to try to restore the situation on his right, word arrived that the next division on his left had collapsed as well and that the Yankees were charging his line in front harder than ever. The division collapsed from both ends and half a dozen places along its line at the same time. As the line went to pieces in the stampede of every man to avoid a Yankee prison if he could, Bragg rode among the fleeing troops, trying to rally them. "I am here. Stop, don't disgrace yourselves, fight for your country!" That sort of thing, from an army commander who waded into the midst of the action like this, usually inspired the men to extraordinary courage, but the Army of Tennessee's morale and confidence in its commander had been undermined too thoroughly for that. "Here's your commander!" Bragg shouted to another flock of fleeing soldiers. "Here's your mule!" replied one of them, quoting the stock punch line of Civil War soldiers' jokes. Seeing the hopelessness of the situation, Bragg rode off down the back side of the ridge with his men. It was 4:30 P.M., less than one hour after the bugles had sent the Army of the Cumberland forward.

Sheridan's troops now swept over the crest, jubilantly celebrating their victory. Colonel Charles G. Harker, another of the heroes of Chickamauga, was enraptured at his brigade's success in capturing a battery of Rebel guns. Exultantly he leapt off his horse and straddled one of the cannons instead, waving his sword and yelling wildly. His men shortly realized the reason for at least some of his yelling as well as his surprisingly rapid dismount from the captured gun—the battery had been firing frantically for forty-five minutes and the tubes were still red-hot.

As Union troops exploited the breakthrough and moved northward along the ridge they encountered, as darkness closed over the landscape, solid resistance from an unbroken Confederate battle line. These were troops of Hardee's Corps, and they fell back in good order covering the Confederate retreat. Once again, Cleburne and his division played the most prominent role. In the opposite direction along the ridge, however, Union troops discovered something much different. As Thomas's men pressed southward in pursuit of the crumbling Confederate battle line, they encountered Hooker's men doing the same thing from the other direction. At about the same time the Cumberlanders had gone forward that afternoon, Hooker had finally reached Rossville Gap, turned north, and started rolling up the Confederate line as Grant had hoped he would be able to do hours earlier.

Night had fallen, and the Union forces were exhausted, disorganized, and badly in need of supplies, both of ammunition and of food. Little hope existed of a successful pursuit—it simply had not been that sort of a battle—but aggressive commanders, especially Phil Sheridan, did press on through the night, forcing Bragg's rear guard to do its job all the way to the crossing of Chickamauga Creek. Bragg still possessed Hardee's unbroken divisions and was able to hold his tormentors at bay. Sheridan had to content himself with a few hundred more prisoners and a few more captured guns.

The next day, Thursday, November 26, 1863, was America's first national Thanksgiving Day. News of the victory at Chattanooga making its way over the telegraph wires provided even more for which Northerners could thank God, after the victories of the summer at Gettysburg and Vicksburg. Grant's soldiers might have been thankful too, but celebration would have to wait. Most of them spent the twenty-sixth once again slogging through mud as the weather shifted to rain, fog, sleet, and ice. Burnside would have to wait up at Knoxville; Grant wanted another piece of Bragg. Unfortunately the piece he got, on November 27, was Cleburne's Division ensconced in another one of those tricky pieces of terrain, this time at a narrow defile called Ringgold Gap, along the Confederate line of retreat. The commander of the Union advance guard quite properly opted to attack at once, not waiting for reinforcements or artillery to come up, since extreme haste was the only way of doing further damage to the enemy. Cleburne, however, was ready and administered a severe and bloody check to Grant's pursuit.

After that setback, accomplishing anything by pursuing Bragg would have meant virtually launching a brand-new campaign, and that Grant simply could not do, much as he may have wanted to. He lacked supplies, and the Army of the Cumberland was all but devoid of horses capable of pulling its artillery and supply wagons—lingering results of the starving times in Chattanooga before Grant took command. Besides, there was Burnside. If Grant might have liked to forget about him, Lincoln certainly was not going to let him. Grant's sensitivity to the political concerns of his civilian superior, the president, was one of the many things that distinguished him above other Union generals. Lincoln wanted help for Burnside—now—and Grant, however reluctantly, would send it. Canceling the pursuit of Bragg, Grant sent Sherman with several divisions on a grueling forced march to Knoxville. He and Sherman were probably not all that surprised when the latter learned that Burnside's situation was nowhere near as bad as Washington had supposed. Still, East Tennessee was now thoroughly secure, and after all, politics were also part of the war.

The Chattanooga campaign was over. Braxton Bragg was ruined, and his government quickly removed him. His army, soon to be commanded by Joseph E. Johnston, retreated to Dalton, Georgia, and there spent the winter. The Confederacy could perhaps afford the forty pieces of artillery lost in the fighting around Chattanooga or even the 6,667 men the battle cost the Army of Tennessee, though the latter, especially, was a heavy blow to scant Southern manpower. Yet most of all the South had needed desperately to reverse the tide of the war after the defeat at Gettysburg and the continuous series of losses in the West that had already cost the Confederacy most of Tennessee and all of Kentucky (to the extent it had ever possessed that state) as well as most of Louisiana and Mississippi. The great concentration of forces in the Army of Tennessee in the fall of 1863 had been an attempt to create just that sort of turn-around, and while Bragg's grip on Chattanooga lasted, it appeared that it just might work. Now such hopes were demolished. The gateway city of the southeast was in Union hands, the South's mountain barrier had been breached, and the way lay open for further Northern advances on a scale far larger than before.

The victory at Chattanooga catapulted Grant to a position of national reputation from which Congress and President Lincoln selected him to be the nation's first full lieutenant general since Washington and overall commander of the Union's armies for the following year's campaign. His relentless, driving style of warfare, guided by his keen political understanding and sound strategic sense, would now characterize the Northern war effort in the final push for victory. Among those who would be his chief lieutenants in that effort, several were present at Chattanooga. Thomas, skillful but slow and contrary, would play an important but limited role. The hard-hitting Sheridan would play a more important part. Sherman, whose Chattanooga performance had been a disappointment, nevertheless kept Grant's confidence. Grant knew him well enough to appreciate the difficult circumstances he had faced. Sherman, moreover, was a man Grant could work with, a man he trusted and who trusted him. He would accept Grant's program and push it vigorously. It thus surprised no one when Grant, upon his elevation to overall Union command, turned over his command in the western theater to Sherman. When spring rolled around to the North Georgia hills again, it would be the red-headed general from Ohio who led the Union's Western armies against Joe Johnston and the Army of Tennessee at Dalton. The stage was thus set for the advance toward Atlanta and the March to the Sea.

Note: The Tables of organization presented in Appendices A and B are taken from War of the Rebellion: Official Records of the Union and Confederate Armies, Series I, Volume 31, Part 2, Pages 14-24 and 656-664. Republished by the National Historical Society, 1972.

APPENDIX A

ORGANIZATION OF FEDERAL FORCES
COMMANDER, MILITARY DIVISION OF THE MISSISSIPPI
MAJ. GEN. ULYSSES S. GRANT

ARMY OF THE CUMBERLAND
MAJ. GEN. GEORGE H. THOMAS

GENERAL HEADQUARTERS
1ST OHIO SHARPSHOOTERS, CAPT. GERSHOM M. BARBER
10TH OHIO INFANTRY, LIEUT. COL. WILLIAM M. WARD

FOURTH ARMY CORPS
MAJ. GEN. GORDON GRANGER

FIRST DIVISION
BRIG. GEN. CHARLES CRUFT

ESCORT
92D ILLINOIS, COMPANY E, CAPT. MATHEW VAN BUSKIRK

Second Brigade
BRIG. GEN. WALTER C. WHITAKER
96th Illinois, Col. Thomas E. Champion
35th Indiana, col. Bernard F. Mullen
8th Kentucky, Col. Sidney M. Barnes
40th Ohio, Col. Jacob E. Taylor
51st Ohio, Lieut. Col. Charles H. Wood
99th Ohio, Lieut. Col. John E. Cummins

Third Brigade
COL. WILLIAM GROSE

59th Illinois, Maj. Clayton Hale
75th Illinois, Col. John E. Bennett
84th Illinois, Col. Louis H. Waters
9th Indiana, Col. Isaac C. B. Suman
36th Indiana, Maj. Gilbert Trusler
24th Ohio, Capt. George M. Bacon

SECOND DIVISION
MAJ. GEN. PHILIP H. SHERIDAN

First Brigade
COL. FRANCIS T. SHERMAN

36th Illinois, Col. Silas Miller
44th Illinois, Col. Wallace W. Barrett
73d Illinois, Col. James F. Jaquess
74th Illinois, Col. Jason Marsh
88th Illinois, Lieut. Col. George W. Chandler
22d Indiana, Col. Michael Gooding
2d Missouri, Col. Bernard Laiboldt
15th Missouri, Col. Joseph Conrad
24th Wisconsin, Maj. Carl von Baumbach

Second Brigade
BRIG. GEN. GEORGE D. WAGNER

100th Illinois, Maj. Charles M. Hammond
15th Indiana, Col. Gustavus A. Wood
40th Indiana, Lieut. Col. Elias Neff
51st Indiana,1 Lieut. Col. John M. Comparet
57th Indiana, Lieut. Col. George W. Lennard
58th Indiana, Lieut. Col. Joseph Moore
26th Ohio, Lieut. Col. William H. Young
97th Ohio, Lieut. Col. Milton Barnes

Third Brigade
COL. CHARLES G. HARKER

22d Illinois, Lieut. Col. Francis Swanwick
27th Illinois, Col. Jonathan R. Miles
42d Illinois, Col. Nathan H. Walworth

51st Illinois, Maj. Charles W. Davis
79th Illinois, Col. Allen Buckner
3d Kentucky, Col. Henry C. Dunlap
64th Ohio, Col. Alexander McIlvain
65th Ohio, Lieut. Col. William A. Bullitt
125th Ohio, Col. Emerson Opdycke

Artillery
CAPT. WARREN P. EDGARTON
1st Illinois Light, Battery M, Capt. George W. Spencer
10th Indiana Battery, Capt. William A. Naylor
1st Missouri Light, Battery G, Lieut. Gustavus Schueler
1st Ohio Light, Battery I, Capt. Hubert Dilger
4th United States, Battery G, Lieut. Christopher F. Merkle
5th United States, Battery H, Capt. Francis L. Guenther

THIRD DIVISION
BRIG. GEN. THOMAS J. WOOD

First Brigade
BRIG. GEN. AUGUST WILLICH
25th Illinois, Col. Richard H. Nodine
35th Illinois, Lieut. Col. William P. Chandler
89th Illinois, Lieut. Col. William D. Williams
32d Indiana, Lieut. Col. Frank Erdelmeyer
68th Indiana, Lieut. Col. Harvey J. Espy
8th Kansas, Col. John A. Martin
15th Ohio, Lieut. Col. Frank Askew
49th Ohio, Maj. Samuel F. Gray
15th Wisconsin, Capt. John A. Gordon

Second Brigade
Brig. Gen. William B. Hazen
6th Indiana, Maj. Calvin D. Campbell
5th Kentucky, Col. William W. Berry
6th Kentucky, Maj. Richard T. Whitaker
23d Kentucky, Lieut. Col. James C. Foy
1st Ohio, Lieut. Col. Bassett Langdon
6th Ohio, Lieut. Col. Alexander C. Christopher
41st Ohio, Col. Aquila Wiley
93d Ohio, Maj. William Birch
124th Ohio, Lieut. Col. James Pickands

Third Brigade

BRIG. GEN. SAMUEL BEATTY

79th Indiana, Col. Frederick Knefler
86th Indiana, Col. George F. Dick
9th Kentucky, Col. George H. Cram
17th Kentucky, Col. Alexander M. Stout
13th Ohio, Col. Dwight Jarvis, jr.
19th Ohio, Col. Charles F. Manderson
59th Ohio, Maj. Robert J. Vanosdol

Artillery

CAPT. CULLEN BRADLEY

Illinois Light, Bridges' Battery, Capt. Lyman Bridges
6th Ohio Battery, Lieut. Oliver H. P. Ayres
20th Ohio Battery, Capt. Edward Grosskopff
Pennsylvania Light, Battery B, Lieut. Samuel M. McDowell

ELEVENTH ARMY CORPS

MAJ. GEN. OLIVER O. HOWARD

GENERAL HEADQUARTERS

INDEPENDENT COMPANY, 8TH NEW YORK INFANTRY, CAPT. ANTON BRUHN

SECOND DIVISION

BRIG. GEN. ADOLPH VON STEINWEHR

First Brigade

COL. ADOLPHUS BUSCHBECK

33d new Jersey, Col. George W. Mindil
134th New York, Lieut. Col. Allan H. Jackson
154th New York, Col. Patrick H. Jones
27th Pennsylvania, Maj. Peter A. McAloon
73d Pennsylvania, Lieut. Col. Joseph B. Taft

Second Brigade

COL. ORLAND SMITH

33d Massachusetts, Lieut. Col. Godfrey Rider, jr.
136th New York, Col. James Wood, jr.
55th Ohio, Col. Charles B. Gambee
73d Ohio, Maj. Samuel H. Hunt

THIRD DIVISION
MAJ. GEN. CARL SCHURZ

First Brigade
BRIG. GEN. HECTOR TYNDALE
101st Illinois, Col. Charles H. Fox
45th New York, Maj. Charles Koch
143d New York, Col. Horace Boughton
61st Ohio, Col. Stephen J. McGroarty
82d Ohio, Lieut. Col. David Thomson

Second Brigade
COL. WLADIMIR KRZYZANOWSKI
58th New York, Capt. Michael Esembaux
119th New York, Col. John T. Lockman
141st New York, Col. William K. Logie
26th Wisconsin, Capt. Frederick C. Winkler

Third Brigade
COL. FREDERICK HECKER
80th Illinois, Capt. James Neville
82d Illinois, Lieut. Col. Edward S. Salomon
68th New York, Lieut. Col. Albert von Steinhausen
75th Pennsylvania, Maj. August Ledig

ARTILLERY
Maj. Thomas W. Osborn
1st New York Light, Battery I, Capt. Michael Wiedrich
New York Light, 13th Battery, Capt. William Wheeler
1st Ohio Light, Battery K, Lieut. Nicholas Sahm

TWELFTH ARMY CORPS
SECOND DIVISION
BRIG. GEN. JOHN W. GEARY

First Brigade
COL. CHARLES CANDY
5th Ohio, Col. John H. Patrick
7th Ohio, Col. William R. Creighton
29th Ohio, Col. William T. Fitch
66th Ohio, Lieut. Col. Eugene Powell
28th Pennsylvania, Col. Thomas J. Ahl
147th Pennsylvania, Lieut. Col. Ario Pardee, jr.

Second Brigade
COL. GEORGE A. COBHAM, JR.
29th Pennsylvania, Col. William Rickards, jr.
109th Pennsylvania, Capt. Frederick L. Gimber
111th Pennsylvania, Col. Thomas M. Walker

Third Brigade
COL. DAVID IRELAND
60th New York, Col. Abel Godard
78th New York, Lieut. Col. Herbert von Hammerstein
102d New York, Col. James C. Lane
137th New York, Capt. Milo B. Eldredge
149th New York, Col. Henry A. Barnum

ARTILLERY
MAJ. JOHN A. REYNOLDS
Pennsylvania Light, Battery E. Lieut. James D. McGill
5th United States, Battery K, Capt. Edmund C. Bainbridge

FOURTEENTH ARMY CORPS
MAJ. GEN. JOHN M. PALMER

ESCORT
1ST OHIO CAVALRY, COMPANY L, CAPT. JOHN D. BARKER

FIRST DIVISION
BRIG. GEN. RICHARD W. JOHNSON

First Brigade
BRIG. GEN. WILLIAM P. CARLIN
104th Illinois, Lieut. Col. Douglas Hapeman
38th Indiana, Lieut. Col. Daniel F. Griffin
42d Indiana, Lieut. Col. William T. B. McIntire
88th Indiana, Col. Cyrus E. Briant
2d Ohio, Col. Anson G. McCook
33d Ohio, Capt. James H. M. Montgomery
94th Ohio, Maj. Rue P. Hutchins
10th Wisconsin, Capt. Jacob W. Roby

Second Brigade
COL. MARSHALL F. MOORE
19th Illinois, Lieut. Col. Alexander W. Raffen
11th Michigan, Capt. Patrick H. Keegan
69th Ohio, Maj. James J. Hanna
15th United States, 1st Battalion, Capt. Henry Keteltas
15th United States, 2d Battalion, Capt. William S. McManus
16th United States, 1st Battalion, Maj. Robert E. A. Crofton
18th United States, 2d Battalion, Capt. Henry Haymond
19th United States, 1st Battalion, Capt. Henry S. Welton

Third Brigade
BRIG. GEN. JOHN C. STARKWEATHER
24th Illinois, Col. Geza Mihalotzy
37th Indiana, Col. James S. Hull
21st Ohio, Capt. Charles H. Vantine
74th Ohio, Maj. Joseph Fisher
78th Pennsylvania, Jam. Augustus B. Bonnaffon
79th Pennsylvania, Maj. Michael H. Locher
1st Wisconsin, Lieut. Col. George B. Bingham
21st Wisconsin, Capt. Charles H. Walker

Artillery
1st Illinois Light, Battery C, Capt. Mark H. Prescott
1st Michigan Light, Battery A, Capt. Francis E. Hale

SECOND DIVISION
BRIG. GEN. JEFFERSON C. DAVIS

First Brigade
BRIG. GEN. JAMES D. MORGAN
10th Illinois, Col. John Tillson
16th Illinois, Lieut. Col. James B. Cahill
60th Illinois, Col. William B. Anderson
21st Kentucky, Col. Samuel W. Price
10th Michigan, Lieut. Col. Christopher J. Dickerson
14th Michigan, 3 Col. Henry R. Mizner

Second Brigade
BRIG. GEN. JOHN BEATTY
34th Illinois, Lieut. Col. Oscar Van Tassell
78th Illinois, Lieut. Col. Carter Van Vleck
3d Ohio, Capt. Leroy S. Bell
98th Ohio, Maj. James M. Shane
108th Ohio, Lieut. Col. Carlo Piepho
113th Ohio, Maj. Lyne S. Sullivant
121st Ohio, Maj. John Yager

Third Brigade
COL. DANIEL MCCOOK
85th Illinois,. Col. Caleb J. Dilworth
86th Illinois, Lieut. Col. David W. Magee
110th Illinois, Lieut. Col. E. Hibbard Topping
125th Illinois,. Col. Oscar F. Harmon
52d Illinois, Maj. James T. Holmes

Artillery
CAPT. WILLIAM A. HOTCHKISS
2d Illinois Light, Battery I, Lieut. Henry B. Plant
Minnesota Light, 2d Battery, Lieut. Richard L. Dawley
Wisconsin Light, 5th Battery, Capt. George Q. Gardner

THIRD DIVISION
Brig. Gen. Absalom Baird

First Brigade
Brig. Gen. John B. Turchin
82d Indiana, Col. Morton C. Hunter
11th Ohio, Lieut. Col. Ogden Street
17th Ohio, Maj. Benjamin F. Butterfield
31st Ohio, Lieut. Col. Frederick W. Lister
36th Ohio, Lieut. Col. Hiram F. Devol
89th Ohio, Capt. John H. Jolly
92d Ohio, Lieut. Col. Douglas Putnam, jr.

Second Brigade
Col. Ferdinand Van Derveer
75th Indiana, Col. Milton S. Robinson
87th Indiana, Col. Newell Gleason
101st Indiana, Lieut. Col. Thomas Doan
2d Minnesota, Lieut. Col. Judson W. Bishop
9th Ohio, Col. Gustave Kamerling
35th Ohio, Lieut. Col. Henry V. N. Boynton
105th Ohio, Lieut. Col. William R. Tolles

Third Brigade
Col. Edward H. Phelps
10th Indiana, Lieut. Col. Marsh B. Taylor
74th Indiana, Lieut. Col. Myron Baker
4th Kentucky, Maj. Robert M. Kelly
10th Kentucky, Col. William H. Hays
18th Kentucky,4 Lieut. Col. Hubbard K. Milward
14th Ohio, Lieut. Col. Henry D. Kingsbury
38th Ohio, Maj. Charles Greenwood

Artillery
Capt. George R. Swallow
Indiana Light, 7th Battery, Lieut. Otho H. Morgan
Indiana Light, 19th Battery, Lieut. Robert G. Lackey
4th United States, Battery I, Lieut. Frank G. Smith

ENGINEER TROOPS
BRIG. GEN. WILLIAM F. SMITH

Engineers
1st Michigan Engineers (detachment), Capt. Perrin V. Fox
13th Michigan Infantry, Maj. Willard G. Eaton
21st Michigan Infantry, Capt. Loomis K. Bishop
22d Michigan Infantry, Maj. Henry S. Dean
18th Ohio Infantry, Col. Timothy R. Stanley

Pioneer Brigade
COL. GEORGE P. BUELL
1st Battalion, Capt. Charles J. Stewart
2d Battalion, Capt. Correll Smith
3d Battalion, Capt. William Clark

ARTILLERY RESERVE
BRIG. GEN. JOHN M. BRANNAN

FIRST DIVISION
COL. JAMES BARNETT

First Brigade
MAJ. CHARLES S. COTTER
1st Ohio Light, Battery B, Lieut. Norman A. Baldwin
1st Ohio Light, Battery C, Capt. Marco B. Gary
1st Ohio Light, Battery E, Lieut. Albert G. Ransom
1st Ohio Light, Battery F, Lieut. Giles J. Cockerill

Second Brigade
1st Ohio Light, Battery G, Capt. Alexander Marshall
1st Ohio Light, Battery M, Capt. Frederick Schultz
Ohio Light, 18th Battery, Lieut. Joseph McCafferty

SECOND DIVISION

First Brigade
CAPT. JOSIAH W. CHURCH
1st Michigan Light, Battery D, Capt. Josiah W. Church
1st Tennessee Light, Battery A, Lieut. Albert F. Beach

Wisconsin Light, 3d Battery, Lieut. Hiram F. Hubbard
Wisconsin Light, 8th Battery, Lieut. Obadiah German
Wisconsin Light, 10th Battery, Capt. Yates V. Beebee

Second Brigade
CAPT. ARNOLD SUTERMEISTER

Indiana Light, 4th Battery, Lieut. Henry J. Willits
Indiana Light, 8th Battery, Lieut. George Estep
Indiana Light, 11th Battery, Capt. Arnold Sutermeister
Indiana Light, 21st Battery, Lieut. William E. Chess
1st Wisconsin Heavy, Company C, Capt. John R. Davies

CAVALRY

SECOND BRIGADE (SECOND DIVISION)
COL. ELI LONG

98th Illinois (mounted infantry), Lieut. Col. Edward Kitchell
17th Indiana (mounted infantry), Lieut. Col. Henry Jordan
2d Kentucky, Col. Thomas P. Nicholas
4th Michigan, Maj. Horace Gray
1st Ohio, Maj. Thomas J. Patten
3d Ohio, Lieut. Col. Charles B. Seidel
4th Ohio (battalion), Maj. George W. Dobb
10th Ohio, Col. Charles C. Smith

POST OF CHATTANOOGA
COL. JOHN G. PARKHURST

44th Indiana, Lieut. Col. Simeon C. Aldrich
15th Kentucky, Maj. William G. Halpin
9th Michigan, Lieut. Col. William Wilkinson

ARMY OF THE TENNESSEE
MAJ. GEN. WILLIAM T. SHERMAN

FIFTEENTH ARMY CORPS
MAJ. GEN. FRANK P. BLAIR, JR.

FIRST DIVISION
BRIG. GEN. PETER J. OSTERHAUS

First Brigade
BRIG. GEN. CHARLES R. WOODS

13th Illinois, Lieut. Col. Frederick W. Partridge
3d Missouri, Lieut. Col. Theodore Meumann
12th Missouri,. Col. Hugo Wangelin
17th Missouri,. Col. John F. Cramer
27th Missouri,. Col. Thomas Curly
29th Missouri,. Col. James Peckham
31st Missouri, Lieut. Col. Samuel P. Simpson
32d Missouri, Lieut. Col. Henry C. Warmoth
76th Ohio, Maj. Willard Warner

Second Brigade
COL. JAMES A. WILLIAMSON

4th Iowa, Lieut. Col. George Burton
9th Iowa,. Col. David Carskaddon
25th Iowa,. Col. George A. Stone
26th Iowa,. Col. Milo Smith
30th Iowa, Lieut. Col. Aurelius Roberts
31st Iowa, Lieut. Col. Jeremiah W. Jenkins

Artillery
CAPT. HENRY H. GRIFFITHS

Iowa Light, 1st Battery, Lieut. James M. Williams
2d Missouri Light, Battery F, Capt. Clemens Landgraeber
Ohio Light, 4th Battery, Capt. George Froehlich

SECOND DIVISION
BRIG. GEN. GILES A. SMITH

First Brigade
BRIG. GEN. GILES A. SMITH
55th Illinois, Col. Oscar Malmborg
116th Illinois, Col. Nathan W. Tupper
127th Illinois, Lieut. Col. Frank S. Curtiss
6th Missouri, Lieut. Col. Ira Boutell
8th Missouri, Lieut. Col. David C. Coleman
57th Ohio, Lieut. Col. Samuel R. Mott
13th United States, 1st Battalion, Capt. Charles C. Smith

Second Brigade
BRIG. GEN. JOSEPH A. J. LIGHTBURN
83d Indiana, Col. Benjamin J. Spooner
30th Ohio, Col. Theodore Jones
37th Ohio, Lieut. Col. Louis von Blessingh
47th Ohio, Col. Augustus C. Parry
54th Ohio, Maj. Robert Williams, jr.
4th West Virginia, Col. James H. Dayton

Artillery
1st Illinois Light, Battery A, Cpat. Peter P. Wood
1st Illinois Light, Battery B, Capt. Israel P. Rumsey
1st Illinois Light, Battery H, Lieut. Francis De Gress

FOURTH DIVISION
BRIG. GEN. HUGH EWING

First Brigade
COL. JOHN M. LOOMIS
26th Illinois, Lieut. Col. Robert A. Gillmore
90th Illinois, Col. Timothy O'Meara
12th Indiana, Col. Reuben Williams
100th Indiana, Lieut. Col. Albert Heath

Second Brigade
BRIG. GEN. JOHN M. CORSE
40th Illinois, Maj. Hiram W. Hall
103d Illinois, Col. Willard A. Dickerman
6th Iowa, lieut. Col. Alexander J. Miller
15th Michigan,5 Lieut. Col. Austin E. Jaquith
46th Ohio, Col. Charles C. Walcutt

Third Brigade
COL. JOSEPH R. COCKERILL
48th Illinois, Lieut. Col. Lucien Greathouse
97th Indiana, Col. Robert F. Catterson
99th Indiana, Col. Alexander Fowler
53d Ohio, Col. Wells S. Jones
70th Ohio, Maj. William B. Brown

Artillery
CAPT. HENRY RICHARDSON
1st Illinois Light, Battery F, Capt. John T. Cheney
1st Illinois Light, Battery I, Lieut. Josiah H. Burton
1st Missouri Light, Battery D, Lieut. Byron M. Callender

SEVENTEENTH ARMY CORPS

SECOND DIVISION
BRIG. GEN. JOHN E. SMITH

First Brigade
COL. JESSE I. ALEXANDER
63d Illinois, Col. Joseph B. McCown
48th Indiana, Lieut. Col. Edward J. Wood
59th Indiana, Capt. Wilford H. Welman
4th Minnesota, Lieut. Col. John E. Tourtellotte
18th Wisconsin, Col. Gabriel Bouck

Second Brigade
COL. GREEN B. RAUM
56th Illinois, Maj. Pinckney J. Welsh
17th Iowa, Col. Clark R. Wever
10th Missouri, Col. Francis C. Deimling
24th Missouri, Company E, Capt. William W. McCammon
80th Ohio, Lieut. Col. Pren Metham

Third Brigade
BRIG. GEN. CHARLES L. MATTHIES
93d Illinois, Col. Holden Putnam
5th Iowa, Col. Jabez Banbury
10th Iowa, Lieut. Col. Paris P. Henderson
26th Missouri, Col. Benjamin D. Dean

Artillery
CAPT. HENRY DILLON
Cogswell's (Illinois) Battery, Capt. William Cogswell
Wisconsin Light, 6th Battery, Lieut. Samuel F. Clark
Wisconsin Light, 12th Battery, Capt. William Zickerick

APPENDIX B

ORGANIZATION OF CONFEDERATE FORCES

ARMY OF TENNESSEE
GEN. BRAXTON BRAGG

GENERAL HEADQUARTERS
1ST LOUISIANA (REGULARS), [COL. JAMES STRAWBRIDGE]
1ST LOUISIANA CAVALRY, [MAJ. J.M. TAYLOR]

HARDEE'S ARMY CORPS
LIEUT. GEN. WILLIAM J. HARDEE

CHEATHAM'S DIVISION
MAJ. GEN. BENJAMIN F. CHEATHAM

Jackson's Brigade
BRIG. GEN. JOHN K. JACKSON
1st Georgia (Confederate), Maj. James C. Gordon
5th Georgia, Col. Charles P. Daniel
47th Georgia, Capt. J.J. Harper
65th Georgia, Lieut. Col. Jacob W. Pearcy
2d Georgia Battalion Sharpshooters,
    Lieut. Col. Richard H. Whiteley
5th Mississippi, Maj. John B. Herring
8th Mississippi, Maj. John F. Smith
37th Alabama, Col. James F. Dowdell
40th Alabama, Col. John H. Higley
42d Alabama, Lieut. Col. Thomas C. Lanier

Walthall's Brigade
BRIG. GEN. EDWARD C. WALTHALL
24th and 27th Mississippi, Col. William F. Dowd
29th and 30th Mississippi, Capt. W.G. Reynolds
34th Mississippi, Col. Samuel Benton

Wright's Brigade
BRIG. GEN. MARCUS J. WRIGHT

8th Tennessee, Col. John H. Anderson
16th Tennessee, Col. D.M. Donnell
28th Tennessee, Col. Sidney S. Stanton
38th Tennessee, Lieut. Col. Andrew D. Gwynne
51st and 52d Tennessee, Lieut. Col. John G. Hall
Murray's (Tennessee) Battalion, Lieut. Col. Andrew D. Gwynne

Artillery Battalion
MAJ. MELANCTHON SMITH

Alabama Battery, Capt. William H. Fowler
Florida Battery, Capt. Robert P. McCants
Georgia Battery, Capt. John Scogin
Mississippi Battery (Smith's), Lieut. William B. Turner

HINDMAN'S DIVISION
BRIG. GEN. PATTON ANDERSON

Anderson's Brigade
COL. W. F. TUCKER

7th Mississippi, Col. William H. Bishop
9th Mississippi, Maj. Thomas H. Lynam
10th Mississippi, Capt. Robert A. Bell
41st Mississippi, Col. W.F. Tucker
44th Mississippi, Lieut. Col. R. G. Kelsey
9th Mississippi Battalion Sharpshooters, Capt. W.W. Tucker

Manigault's Brigade
BRIG. GEN. ARTHUR MANIGAULT

24th Alabama, Col. N.N. Davis
28th Alabama, Maj. W.L. Butler
34th Alabama, Maj. John N. Slaughter
10th and 19th South Carolina, Maj. James L. White

Deas' Brigade
BRIG. GEN. ZACHARIAH C. DEAS

19th Alabama, Col. Samuel K. McSpadden
22d Alabama, Capt. Harry T. Toulmin
25th Alabama, Col. George D. Johnston

39th Alabama, Col. Whitfield Clark
50th Alabama, Col. J.G. Coltart
17th Alabama Battalion Sharpshooters, Capt. James F. Nabors

Vaughan's Brigade
BRIG. GEN. ALFRED VAUGHAN
11th Tennessee, Col. George W. Gordon
12th and 47th Tennessee, Col. William M. Watkins
13th and 154th Tennessee, Lieut. Col. R.W. Pitman
29th Tennessee, Col. Horace Rice

Artillery Battalion
MAJ. ALFRED R. COURTNEY
Alabama Battery, Capt. S.H. Dent
Alabama Battery, Capt. James Garrity
Tennessee Battery (Scott's), Lieut. John Doscher
Alabama Battery (Water's), Lieut. William P. Hamilton

BUCKNER'S DIVISION
MAJ. GEN. SIMON B. BUCKNER

Johnson's Brigade
BRIG. GEN. BUSHROD R. JOHNSON
17th and 23d Tennessee, Lieut. Col. Watt W. Floyd
25th and 44th Tennessee, Lieut. Col. John L. McEwen, jr.
63d Tennessee, Maj. John A. Aiken

Gracie's Brigade
BRIG. GEN. ARCHIBALD GRACIE
41st Alabama, Lieut. Col. Theodore G. Trimmier
43d Alabama, Col. Young M. Moody
1st Battalion, Alabama (Hilliard's) Legion, Maj. Daniel S. Troy
2d Battalion, Alabama (Hilliard's) Legion, Capt. John H. Dillard
3d Battalion, Alabama (Hilliard's) Legion,
     Lieut. Col. John W.A. Sanford
4th Battalion, Alabama (Hilliard's) Legion,
     Maj. John D. McLennan

Reynolds' Brigade
BRIG. GEN. A. W. REYNOLDS
58th North Carolina, Col. John B. Palmer
60th North Carolina, Capt. James T. Weaver
54th Virginia, Lieut. Col. John J. Wade
63d Virginia, Maj. James M. French

Artillery Battalion
MAJ. SAMUEL C. WILLIAMS
Mississippi Battery (Darden's), Lieut. H.W. Bullen
Virginia Battery, Capt. William C. Jeffress
Alabama Battery, Capt. R.F. Kolb

WALKER'S DIVISION
MAJ. GEN. WILLIAM H.T. WALKER

Maney's Brigade
BRIG. GEN. GEORGE MANEY
1st and 27th Tennessee, Col. Hume R. Field
4th Tennessee (Provisional Army), Capt. Joseph Bostick
6th and 9th Tennessee, Lieut. Col. J.W. Buford
41st Tennessee, Col. Robert Farquharson
50th Tennessee, Col. Cyrus A. Sugg
24th Tennessee Battalion Sharpshooters, Maj. Frank Maney

Gist's Brigade
BRIG. GEN. STATES RIGHTS GIST
46th Georgia, Lieut. Col. William A. Daniel
8th Georgia Battalion, Lieut. Col. Leroy Napier
16th South Carolina, Col. James McCullough
24th South Carolina, Col. Clement H. Stevens

Wilson's Brigade
COL. CLAUDIUS C. WILSON
25th Georgia, Col. Claudius C. Wilson
29th Georgia, Col. William J. Young
30th Georgia, Col. Thomas W. Mangham
26th Georgia Battalion, Maj. John W. Nisbet
1st Georgia Battalion Sharpshooters, Maj. Arthur Shaaff

Artillery Battalion
MAJ. ROBERT MARTIN
Missouri Battery, Capt. Hiram M. Bledsoe
South Carolina Battery, Capt. T.B. Ferguson
Georgia Battery, Capt. Evan P. Howell

BRECKINRIDGE'S ARMY CORPS
MAJ. GEN. JOHN C. BRECKINRIDGE

CLEBURNE'S DIVISION
MAJ. GEN. PATRICK R. CLEBURNE

Liddell's Brigade
2d and 15th Arkansas, Maj. E. Warfield
5th and 13th Arkansas, Col. John E. Murray
6th and 7th Arkansas, Lieut. Col. Peter Snyder
8th Arkansas, Maj. Anderson Watkins
19th and 24th Arkansas, Lieut. Col. A.S. Hutchinson

Smith's Brigade
BRIG. GEN. JAMES A. SMITH
6th and 10th Texas Infantry and 15th Texas
    (dismounted) Cavalry, Col. Roger Q Mills
7th Texas, Col. Hiram B. Granbury
17th, 18th, 24th, and 25th Texas Cavalry (dismounted),
    Maj. William A. Taylor

Polk's Brigade
BRIG. GEN. LUCIUS POLK
1st Arkansas, Col. John W. Colquitt
3d and 5th Confederate, Lieut. Col. J.C. Cole
2d Tennessee, Col. William D. Robinson
35th and 48th Tennessee, Col. Benjamin J. Hill

Lowrey's Brigade
BRIG. GEN. MARK P. LOWREY
16th Alabama, Maj. Frederick A. Ashford
33d Alabama, Col. Samuel Adams
45th Alabama, Lieut. Col. H.D. Lampley
32d and 45th Mississippi, Lieut. Col. R. Charlton
15th Mississippi Battalion Sharpshooters, Capt. Daniel Coleman

STEWART'S DIVISION
MAJ. GEN. ALEXANDER P. STEWART

Adam's Brigade
BRIGADIER GENERAL DANIEL W. ADAMS
13th and 20th Louisiana, Col. Leon von Zinken
16th and 25th Louisiana, Col. Daniel Gober
19th Louisiana, Col. W.P. Winans
4th Louisiana Battalion, Lieut. Col. John McEnery
14th Louisiana Battalion Sharpshooters, Maj. J.E. Austin

Strahl's Brigade
BRIG. GEN. OTHO STRAHL
4th and 5th Tennessee, Col. Jonathan J. Lamb
19th Tennessee, Col. Francis M. Walker
24th Tennessee, Col. John A. Wilson
31st Tennessee, Col. Egbert E. Tansil
33d Tennessee, Lieut. Col. Henry C. McNeill

Clayton's Brigade
BRIG. GEN. HENRY D. CLAYTON
18th Alabama, Maj. Shep. Ruffin
32d Alabama, Capt. John W. Bell
36th Alabama, Col. Lewis T. Woodruff
38th Alabama, Col. Charles T. Ketchum
58th Alabama, Lieut. Col. John W. Inzer

Stovall's Brigade
BRIG. GEN. MARCELLUS STOVALL
40th Georgia, [Col. Abda Johnson]
41st Georgia, [Col. William E. Curtiss]
42d Georgia, [Col. R.J. Henderson]
43d Georgia, [Col. Hiram P. Bell]
52d Georgia, [Maj. John J. Moore]

Artillery Battalion
CAPT. HENRY C. SEMPLE
Georgia Battery (Dawson's), Lieut. R.W. Anderson
Arkansas Battery (Humphreys'), Lieut. John W. Rivers
Alabama Battery, Capt. McDonald Oliver
Mississippi Battery, Capt. Thomas J. Stanford

BRECKINRIDGE'S DIVISION
BRIG. GEN. WILLIAM B. BATE

Lewis' Brigade
BRIG. GEN. JOSEPH H. LEWIS
2d Kentucky, Lieut. Col. James W. Moss
4th Kentucky, Maj. Thomas W. Thompson
5th Kentucky, col. H. Hawkins
6th Kentucky, Col. H. Hawkins
9th Kentucky, Lieut. Col. John C. Wickliffe
John H. Morgan's dismounted men

Bate's Brigade
COL. R.C. TYLER
37th Georgia, Col. A.F. Rudler
4th Georgia Battalion Sharpshooters, Lieut. Joel Towers
10th Tennessee, Col. William Grace
15th and 37th Tennessee, Lieut. Col. R. Dudly Frayser
20th Tennessee, Maj. W.M. Shy
30th Tennessee, Lieut. Col. James J. Turner
1st Tennessee Battalion, Maj. Stephen H. Colms

Florida Brigade
COL. JESSE J. FINLEY
1st and 3d Florida, Capt. W.T. Saxon
4th Florida, Lieut. Col. E. Badger
6th Florida, Col. Jesse J. Finley
7th Florida, Lieut. Col. Tillman Ingram
1st Florida Cavalry (dismounted), Col. G. Troup Maxwell

Artillery Battalion
CAPT. C. H. SLOCOMB
Kentucky Battery (Cobb's), Lieut. Frank P. Gracey
Tennessee Battery, Capt. John W. Mebane
Louisiana Battery (Slocomb's), Lieut. W.C.D. Vaught

STEVENSON'S DIVISION
MAJ. GEN. CARTER L. STEVENSON

Brown's Brigade
BRIG. GEN. JOHN C. BROWN
3d Tennessee, Col. Calvin H. Walker
18th and 26th Tennessee, Lieut. Col. William R. Butler
32d Tennessee, Capt. Thomas D. Deavenport
45th Tennessee and 23d Tennessee Battalion,
    Col. Anderson Searcy

Cumming's Brigade
BRIG. GEN. ALFRED CUMMING
34th Georgia, Col. J.A.W. Johnson
36th Georgia, Lieut. Col. Alexander M. Wallace
39th Georgia, Col. J.T. McConnell
56th Georgia, Lieut. Col. J.T. Slaughter

Pettus' Brigade
BRIG. GEN. EDMUND W. PETTUS
20th Alabama, Capt. John W. Davis
23d Alabama, Lieut. Col. J.B. Bibb
30th Alabama, Col. Charles M. Shelley
31st Alabama, Col. D.R. Hundley
46th Alabama, Capt. George E. Brewer

Vaughn's Brigade
BRIG. GEN. JOHN C. VAUGHN
3d Tennessee (Provisional Army)
39th Tennessee
43d Tennessee
59th Tennessee

Artillery Battalion
CAPT. ROBERT COBB
Tennessee Battery, Capt. Edmund D. Baxter
Tennessee Battery, Capt. William W. Carnes
Georgia Battery Capt. Max Van Den Corput
Georgia Battery, Capt. John B. Rowan

WHEELER'S CAVALRY CORPS
MAJ. GEN. JOSEPH WHEELER

WHARTON'S DIVISION
MAJ. GEN. JOHN A. WHARTON

First Brigade
COL. THOMAS HARRISON

3d Arkansas, Lieut. Col. M.J. Henderson
65th North Carolina (6th Cavalry), Col. George N. Folk
8th Texas, Lieut. Col. Gustave Cook
11th Texas, Lieut. Col. J.M. Bounds

Second Brigade
BRIG. GEN. HENRY B. DAVIDSON

1st Tennessee, Col. James E. Carter
2d Tennessee, Col. Henry M. Ashby
4th Tennessee, Col. William S. McLemore
6th Tennessee, Col. James T. Wheeler
11th Tennessee, Col. Daniel W. Holman

MARTIN'S DIVISION
MAJ. GEN. WILLIAM T. MARTIN

First Brigade
BRIG. GEN. JOHN T. MORGAN

1st Alabama, Lieut. Col. D.T. Blakey
3d Alabama, Lieut. Col. T.H. Mauldin
4th Alabama [Russell's], Lieut. Col. J.M. Hambrick
Malone's (Alabama) Regiment, Col. James C. Malone, jr.
51st Alabama, Capt. M.L. Kirkpatrick

Second Brigade
COL. J.J. MORRISON

1st Georgia, Lieut. Col. S.W. Davitte
2nd Georgia, Lieut. Col. F.M. Ison
3d Georgia, Lieut. Col. R. Thompson
4th Georgia, Col. Isaac W. Avery
6th Georgia, Col. John R. Hart

ARMSTRONG'S DIVISION
Brig. Gen. Frank C. Armstrong

First Brigade
Brig. Gen. William Y. C. Humes
4th Tennessee [Baxter Smith's], Lieut. Col. Paul F. Anderson
5th Tennessee, Col. George W. McKenzie
8th Tennessee [Dibrell's],
9th Tennessee, Col. Jacob B. Biffle
10th Tennessee, Col. Nicholas N. Cox

Second Brigade
Col. C. H. Tyler
Clay's (Kentucky) Battalion, Lieut. Col. Ezekiel F. Clay
Edmundson's (Virginia) Battalion, Maj. S.P. McConnell
Jessee's (Kentucky) Battalion, Maj. A.L. McAfee
Johnson's (Kentucky) Battalion, Maj. O.S. Tenney

KELLY'S DIVISION
Brig. Gen. John H. Kelly

First Brigade
Col. William B. Wade
1st Confederate, Capt. C.H. Conner
3d Confederate, Col. W.N. Estes
8th Confederate, Lieut. Col. John S. Prather
10th Confederate, Col. Charles T. Goode

Second Brigade
Col. J. Warren Grigsby
2d Kentucky, Col. Thomas G. Woodward
3d Kentucky, Col. J.R. Butler
9th Kentucky, Col. W.C.P. Breckinridge
Allison's (Tennessee) Squadron, Capt. R.D. Allison
Hamilton's (Tennessee) Battalion, Lieut. Col. O.P. Hamilton
Rucker's Legion, Col. E.W. Rucker

ARTILLERY

TENNESSEE BATTERY, CAPT. A.L. HUGGINS

Tennessee Battery, Capt. Gustave A. Huwald

Tennessee Battery, Capt B.F. White, jr.

Arkansas Battery, Capt. J.H. Wiggins

RESERVE ARTILLERY

MAJ. FELIX H. ROBERTSON

Missouri Battery, Capt. Overton W. Barret

Georgia Battery (Havis'), Lieut. James R. Duncan

Alabama Battery (Lumsden's), Lieut. Harvey H. Cribbs

Georgia Battery, Capt. Thomas L. Massenburg

SELECTED BIBLIOGRAPHY

Alexander, Edward Porter. *Fighting for the Confederacy: The personal Recollections of General Edward Porter Alexander.* Edited by Gary W. Gallagher. Chapel Hill and London: University of North Carolina Press, 1989.

_____. *Military Memoirs of a Confederate.* Reprint. Bloomington: Indiana University Press, 1962.

Arnold, James R. *The Armies of U.S. Grant.* London: Arms and Armour Press, 1995.

Buck, Irving A. *Cleburne and His Command.* Jackson, TN: McCowat-Mercer, 1959.

Catton, Bruce. *Grant Takes Command.* Boston: Little, Brown, 1968.

Connelly, Thomas Lawrence. *Autumn of Glory: The Army of Tennessee, 1862–1865.* Baton Rouge: Louisiana State University Press, 1971.

Connelly, Thomas Lawrence, and Archer Jones, *The Politics of Command: Factions and Ideas in Confederate Strategy.* Baton Rouge: Louisiana State University Press, 1973.

Cozzens, Peter. *The Shipwreck of Their Hopes: The Battle for Chattanooga.* Urbana: University of Illinois Press, 1994.

Cummings, Charles M. *Yankee Quaker, Confederate General: The Curious Career of General Bushrod Rust Johnson.* Cranbury, NJ: Fairleigh Dickinson University Press, 1971.

Davis, William C. *Breckinridge: Statesman, Soldier, Symbol.* Baton Rouge: Louisiana State University Press, 1974.

Eckenrode, H.J. and Bryan Conrad. *James Longstreet: Lee's War Horse.* Reprint. Chapel Hill and London: University of North Carolina Press, 1986.

Franks, Edward Carr. "The Detachment of Longstreet Considered: Braxton Bragg, James Longstreet, and the Chattanooga Campaign," in Steven E. Woodworth, editor. Leadership and Command in the American Civil War. Campbell, CA: Savas Woodbury, 1995.

Hallock, Judith Lee. *Braxton Bragg and Confederate Defeat. Volume II.* Tuscaloosa: University of Alabama Press, 1991.

Hattaway, Herman, and Archer Jones. *How the North Won: A Military History of the Civil War*. Urbana: University of Illinois Press, 1991.

Heck, Frank H. *Proud Kentuckian: John C. Breckinridge, 1821–1875*. Lexington: University Press of Kentucky, 1976.

Horn, Stanley. *The Army of Tennessee*. Indianapolis: Bobbs-Merrill, 1941.

Hughes, Nathaniel Cheairs, Jr. *General William J. Hardee: Old Reliable*. Baton Rouge: Louisiana State University Press, 1965.

Grant, Ulysses S. *Papers of Ulysses S. Grant*. Edited by John Y. Simon. 20 vols to date. Carbondale and Edwardsville: Southern Illinois University Press, 1967–. Volume 9 contains Grant's correspondence during the Chattanooga Campaign.

_____. *Personal memoirs of Ulysses S. Grant*. 2 vols. New York: Charles L. Webster and Company, 1885.

Jackman, John S. *Diary of A Confederate Soldier: John S. Jackman of the Orphan Brigade*. Edited by William C. Davis. Columbia: University of South Carolina Press, 1990.

Johnson, Robert Underwood, and Clarence Clough Buel, eds. *Battles and Leaders of the Civil War*. 4 vols. New York: Thomas Yoseloff, Inc., 1956. Volume 3 contains accounts by participants in the Chattanooga Campaign.

Longstreet, James. *From Manassas to Appomattox: Memoirs of the Civil War in America*. Edited by James I. Robertson, Jr. New ed. Bloomington: Indiana University Press, 1960.

Manigault, Arthur. *A Carolinian Goes to War: The Civil War Narrative of Arthur Middleton Manigault, Brigadier General, C.S.A.* Columbia: University of South Carolina Press, 1983.

Marszalek, John F. *Sherman: A Soldier's Passion for Order*. New York: The Free Press, 1993.

Marvel, William. *Burnside*. Chapel Hill and London: University of North Carolina Press, 1991.

McDonough, James Lee. *Chattanooga: A Death Grip on the Confederacy*. Knoxville: University of Tennessee Press, 1984.

McFeely, William S. *Grant: A Biography*. New York: W.W. Norton and Company, 1981.

McKinney, Francis F. *Education in Violence: George H. Thomas and the History of the Army of the Cumberland.* Detroit: Wayne State University Press, 1961.

Mosman, Chesley A. *The Rough Side of War: The Civil War Journal of Chesley A. Mosman, 1st Lieutenant, Company D, 59th Illinois Volunteer Infantry Regiment.* Edited by Arnold Gates. Garden City, NY: Basin, 1987.

Piston, William Garrett. *Lee's Tarnished Lieutenant: James Longstreet and His Place in Southern History.* Athens and London: University of Georgia Press, 1987.

Porter, Horace. *Campaigning with Grant.* Reprint. Bloomington: Indiana University Press, 1961.

Purdue, Howell, and Elizabeth Purdue, *Pat Cleburne, Confederate General.* Tuscaloosa, AL: Portals Press, 1973.

Seitz, Don C. *Braxton Bragg: General of the Confederacy.* Columbia, SC: The State Company, 1924.

Sherman, William T. *Memoirs of General William T. Sherman.* 2 vols. Reprint. Bloomington: University of Indiana Press, 1957.

Simpson, Brooks D. *Let Us Have Peace: Ulysses S. Grant and the Politics of War and Peace, 1861–1868.* Chapel Hill and London: University of North Carolina Press, 1991.

Sorrel, G. Moxley. *Recollections of a Confederate Staff Officer.* Reprint. Dayton, Ohio: Morningside Bookshop, 1978.

The Story of the Fifty-fifth Illinois Regiment in the Civil War, 1861–1865. By a committee of the regiment. Reprint. Huntington, WV: Blue Acorn Press, 1993.

Sword, Wiley. *Mountains Touched with Fire: Chattanooga Besieged, 1863.* New York: St. Martin's, 1995.

Turner, George Edgar. *Victory Rode the Rails: The Strategic Place of the Railroads in the Civil War.* Reprint. Lincoln: University of Nebraska Press, 1994.

Wert, Jeffry D. *General James Longstreet: The Confederacy's Most Controversial General—A Biography.* New York: Simon & Schuster, 1993.

Wills, Brian Steel. *A Battle from the Start: The Life of Nathan Bedford Forrest.* New York: Harper Collins, 1992.

Wingfield, Marshall. *General A.P. Stewart: His Life and Letters*. Memphis: West Tennessee Historical Society, 1954.

Woodworth, Steven E. *Jefferson Davis and His Generals: The Failure of Confederate Command in the West*. Lawrence: University Press of Kansas, 1990.

_____. *Six Armies in Tennessee: The Chickamauga and Chattanooga Campaigns*. Lincoln: University of Nebraska Press, 1997.

ABOUT THE BIOGRAPHICAL SKETCHES

The biographical sketches that accompany the photographs in this volume were derived from numerous sources and written by Paul Cochran, David Coffey, and Grady McWhiney.

SELECTED REFERENCE WORKS

Boatner, Mark M, III. *The Civil War Dictionary.* Revised edition. New York: David McKay Company, 1988.

Current, Richard N. ed. *Encyclopedia of the Confederacy.* 4 vols. New York: Simon & Schuster, 1993.

Davis, William C. ed. *The Confederate General.* 6 vols. National Historical Society, 1991.

Sifakis, Stewart. *Who Was Who in the Union.* New York: Facts on File, 1988.

_____. *Who Was Who in the Confederacy.* New York: Facts on File, 1988.

Warner, Ezra. *Generals in Gray: Lives of the Confederate Commanders.* Baton Rouge: Louisiana State University Press, 1959.

_____. *Generals in Blue: Lives of the Union Commanders.* Baton Rouge: Louisiana State University Press, 1964.

PHOTO CREDITS

We acknowledge the cooperation of the United States Army Military History Institute at Carlisle Barracks, Pennsylvania for photographs of John C. Breckinridge, Gordon Granger, William J. Hardee, Joseph Hooker, Peter J. Osterhaus, Philip Henry Sheridan, Carter L. Stevenson, and Thomas J. Wood.

We acknowledge the cooperation of the Library of Congress for photographs of Braxton Bragg, Ambrose Everett Burnside, Patrick Cleburne, Ulysses S. Grant, James Longstreet, William T. Sherman, and George H. Thomas.

The photographs of William B. Bate and John K. Jackson were taken from Ezra Warner's *Generals in Gray: Lives of the Confederate Commanders* (Louisiana State University Press, 1959).

INDEX

CPSIA information can be obtained at www.ICGtesting.com
Printed in the USA
LVOW11s1046190614

390795LV00005B/13/P